BLACK FACES,
WHITE S P A C E S

BLACK FACES, WHITE SPACES

Reimagining the Relationship of
African Americans to the Great Outdoors

CAROLYN FINNEY

The University of North Carolina Press *Chapel Hill*

*Publication of this book was assisted by the Wachovia Wells Fargo Fund
for Excellence of the University of North Carolina Press*

© 2014 THE UNIVERSITY OF NORTH CAROLINA PRESS

Library of Congress Cataloging-in-Publication Data
Finney, Carolyn.
Black faces, white spaces : reimagining the relationship of African Americans to
the great outdoors / Carolyn Finney.
  pages cm
Includes bibliographical references and index.
ISBN 978-1-4696-1448-9 (pbk.) — ISBN 978-1-4696-1449-6 (ebook)
 1. African Americans—Social conditions. 2. Human ecology—United States. I. Title.
E185.86.F525 2014
304.2089'96073—dc23
2014000594

18 17 16 15 14 5 4 3 2 1

THIS BOOK WAS DIGITALLY PRINTED.

Contents

Illustrations

Preface

Nothing is more powerful than an idea whose time has come.
—Victor Hugo

You can't get to wonderful without passing through alright.
—Bill Withers, *Wisdom: The Greatest Gift One Generation Can Give to Another*

In March of 2007, I was invited to the University of Vermont to speak to the academic community about the intersection of race and the environment. I had given versions of this talk at other universities where, with the exception of a few historically black colleges in the South, my audience was largely white. While the content of my talks did not change, I always found it interesting the way in which different audiences collectively responded to my assertions about the "black experience" and the mainstream environmental movement in the United States. Whether the audience was predominately white, black, or a mix of diverse individuals, responses were often a combination of surprise, anger, curiosity, and hope. To a lesser extent (and perhaps this is because people were less likely to reveal these feelings in a public setting), I could also sense doubt, denial, and even dismissal. In any case, there was always much back and forth between myself and audience members as we navigated the sometimes emotionally tumultuous waters of race.

Along with sharing some facts and findings from my empirical research, I luxuriated in sharing stories about some of the people I was privileged to have interviewed. I found that personalizing the discussion about race and environment—either with my own stories or the stories of others—was a great way to invite people into the conversation by reminding them that this wasn't just a black, white, or brown experience; it was a *human* experience. At the University of Vermont, I began with one such story. I was especially fond of speaking about John Francis, a man who had spent twenty-two years walking across the United States to raise environmental awareness. On this particular day, I paused after saying "twenty-two years," waiting for the audience to murmur and look simultaneously surprised and impressed. Then, as I usually did, I added the punch line: "And for seventeen of those years, he did it *without talking*." A collective gasp ran through the audience: How is that possible? How did he communicate? Why did he do it? I loved this part—talking to people about how John earned his Ph.D. during this period (without talking), became a representative for the United Nations, and was one of the original architects of our oil spill policy that was instituted after the Exxon Valdez disaster infiltrated our seas and our environmental conversations.

Pleased with myself, I ended this story by sharing how Hollywood was preparing to make a movie about his life. Won't it be amazing, even revolutionary, to see a mainstream movie about a black man walking across America to raise environmental awareness? As I continued talking amid laughs and nods of agreement, a young white woman timidly raised her hand. "Yes?" I smiled. "Well—uh—I'm not sure how to say this, but I have to tell you that as you were telling the story about John Francis, I just assumed he was *white*." Now, this was one of those moments a speaker loves. The young woman's declaration was completely unplanned and unscripted, but it underscored the point I was trying to make in my talk: that we have collectively come to understand/see/envision the environmental debate as shaped and inhabited primarily by white people. And our ability to imagine others is *colored* by the narratives, images, and meanings we've come to hold as truths in relation to the environment. It is not unlike that old joke that challenged gender stereotypes: A boy gets into a bad car accident. The doctor at the hospital says, "I can't operate on this boy, he's my son." When the joke teller asks, "who is the doctor?" we figure the doctor must be the boy's father. Then we find out that he's the boy's mother.

In the case of race and the environment, it's not just who we imagine has something valuable to say. These assumptions, beliefs, and perceptions are at the very foundation of our environmental thinking, how we define the "environment," and how we think of ourselves in relationship with the environment. Who do we see, what do we see? In *Outside* magazine, Eddy Harris, a black writer and self-described outdoorsman, says that we see black people on television as lawyers or doctors, but we balk at imagining African Americans in the great outdoors. Sid Wilson, president of the hiking organization A Private Guide, Inc., in Colorado, agrees. "When we do [see black people in the natural environment in the media], bears start rappin.'"

Television and magazines aren't the only areas where stories about the African American environmental experience reflect our vision-challenged perspective. During the 1980s, the environmental justice movement emerged as a vehicle for addressing social justice concerns and taking on the question of racism. But twenty years later, the mainstream environmental movement is accused of falling short of addressing certain concerns, such as managing to "racially integrate their senior staff" (Gelobter et al. 2005). In every other sector of society, African Americans have made significant strides in becoming visible. No longer needing to be stealthy, we've thrown off the cloak of invisibility in education, music, law, medicine, and politics.[1] For the first time in history, a self-identified African American man has become president. What is happening in the environmental movement? Are African Americans not interested, not involved, too busy with other issues? Is it really, as one black student told me at Tennessee State University, "A white thing"? Are there "exclusionary practices" in place that inhibit greater involvement by black folks? Are we limited in our role as victims in larger narratives (e.g., Hurricane Katrina)? And what of our agency? In the 1960s, two black psychiatrists, William Grier and Price Cobbs, wrote a book called *Black Rage* that explained how black pride and a positive sense of self grew in response to negative depictions and physical limitations imposed on black people by the majority culture. At the same time these psychiatrists contend that we "shrunk our ledge" in imagining who we were and who we could be. Have we shrunk our ledge? Are we content to freefall in the narratives written by others where political correctness and sympathy are meant to substitute for true engagement and relationship?

ON LIVING COLOR

Here I must pause and intervene. My training as a social scientist, and more specifically as a geographer, has provided me with the skills to challenge traditional thinking about the production of knowledge and to think about the relationship between people and the world we live in. I've developed the tools to frame and name processes and phenomena and have taken advantage of opportunities to put my claims in the intellectual mix. However, I cannot in good conscience write this book about interrogating and challenging the way in which the African American environmental relationship gets defined and legitimated in the media and in environmental organizations without first providing you with my intellectual viewpoint and revealing a piece of my own story.[2]

Conceptualizations of the environment, the legitimization of certain definitions, and the shaping of debates are created and constructed by people who, in turn, are informed by their own identity, their life experience, and the context in which they live. In addition, there is power and privilege at work, mediating the process of naming and claiming experiences in the world, setting the tone and the norm by which others are expected to measure themselves. I am offering another interpretation, another way of understanding African Americans and the environment, and I have the power to do this largely because of my academic experience—the skills I've learned that help me think, analyze, and write what I come to know. But the privilege is two-fold: the access I have to opportunities to get my work out there and the privilege of being born black in what seemed a largely white world that had already decided who I was and where my place was before I even learned to walk. I can tell the story with some authority (as a white colleague rightly pointed out) because I have been given the chance to see the world in *living* color on a daily basis.

The questions I ask in this book were informed by academia, cultural studies, geography, and public discourse. But the primary motivation was personal. I was born in New York City during the civil rights era and was adopted by a black couple who had recently migrated north on the well-worn path of black movement coming up from the South. I grew up on a large estate right outside of New York City on twelve scenic, naturally wooded acres, with a large pond and an abundance of oak, beech, apple, and peach trees (Figure 1). My parents were the caretakers: gardener, chauffer, housekeeper, and permanent residents. Material wealth was all around us; there were other large tracts of land, big houses, and famous people that lived in the area (including Harry Winston, the diamond king). Since the owners of our home only came up from the city on weekends and holidays, my brothers and I had our own playground five days a week. And like any family, we grew stories about ourselves in that place. While I came to love what was "natural," I also discovered that for some folks it wasn't "natural" for my family or me to be there. We were the only "colored" family living in this area (and this remained true until the 1990s).

I watched my parents take care of this land every day; they tended the garden, mowed the grass, and chased the geese. I watched my parents care for somebody else's land for fifty years but not be able to claim ownership in any real way. I saw how my parents, with their twelfth-grade education, knew more about that land than the actual owners. But I also realized how this knowledge and commitment did not result in legal ownership of the

Figure 1. The estate/my home. Photograph taken by Finney family.

land. Before the original owners passed away, they tried to arrange it so that my parents could stay on the land. However, the concerns of their adult children and the reality that my parents could never afford the property taxes (amounting to approximately $125,000 a year) meant they could not stay. In looking to my parents and their story, I began to think about land and ownership. Whose land is this, anyway? And is ownership only about a piece of paper, or can it mean something more? Where do my parents fit in the mainstream environmental conversation?

For the past few years, I have been privileged to speak with black, white, and brown Americans across the country about race, racism, the media, and all matters deemed "environmental." In particular, African Americans have shared with me their childhood stories from the woods and the 'hood, the North and the South, and from the 1930s to the 1980s. Whether working on a farm or hanging out on a stoop, their experiences of nature were usually welcomed by them, sometimes challenged by others, and were always bumping up against social, economic, and historical processes that served to remind them that their map of the world, while fluid, demanded a particularly fine-tuned compass that allowed them to navigate a landscape that was not always hospitable.

What I discovered/uncovered/recovered is the many ways in which—be it physical, artistic, or spiritual—black people have laid it all down in order to feed their children, plant their dreams, and share their experience and history with the environment. People like MaVynee Betsch who, in her middle years, gave away all her wealth to environmental causes and fought hard until her death in 2005 to conserve and protect both the natural resources of her home place, American Beach on Amelia Island in Florida, and the African American history that she believed was an intricate part of that landscape. Or Eddy Harris, who at the age of thirty during the 1980s, canoed the length of the Mississippi River to understand both the material and spiritual meaning of the river in American life and to explore what it meant to be a black man in contemporary society. Or Shelton Johnson, a black park ranger in Yosemite National Park who revived the story of the Buffalo soldiers and their role in protecting the park by incorporating the story into the larger park narrative through interpretation, film, and the written word. Or people like my parents who simply wanted to feed their families and provide new opportunities and a better life for their children.

From Wynton Marsalis to Toni Morrison to Will Allen to Majora Carter to a man named Pearl, African Americans toiled, sang songs, wrote stories, and transformed the landscape with hard work, big dreams, and a belief that African Americans have and have always had an intimate, ever-changing and significant relationship with the natural environment. In the following pages, I hope to highlight some of those experiences and the way in which African Americans, both individually and collectively, continue to nurture that connection.

The audience I hope to engage includes academics in a variety of disciplines, practitioners, environmentalists broadly defined, and "just folks" who, like my parents, are working and living in relation to the natural environment every day. As such, I understand that everyone brings different expectations to the table about my approach to writing this book. So I would like to offer some explanation and, if I may be so bold, some guidance and points of reference to my method. In this book, I am attempting to do two things: lay out a rendering of the African American/environmental relationship that reveals some of the contradictions and synergies; and equally attribute the knowledge that comes from nonacademic sites of learning as central to our understanding of the African American environmental relationship, not simply as anecdotal to our comprehension. For me, this requires that I be willing to "sit" in the ambiguity and complexity of the African American environment relationship by engaging multiple sites where black "voicings" reside. In particular, I draw on popular culture, critical race studies, art, African American studies, memoirs, and even music, along with more "traditional" areas of knowledge production such as geography and environmental history. Sometimes I do this quite directly by referencing a well-known film or popular artwork in relation to an idea that I am exploring. Other times, I take a "sideways" approach where I invite the reader to engage a little creative improvisation by considering a phrase or example or reference that doesn't necessarily explain itself so explicitly. For instance, the titles to some of my chapters are references to Spike Lee films. As he is a kind of cultural jedi who uses film to address African American life, his films offer whole worlds of living and knowing that could fill volumes, but that are too substantial to include in these pages. So I take a bit of a shortcut—in my first chapter, titled "Bamboozled" I am referencing his film where he highlights the hypocrisies, contradictions, and misrepresentations concerning African Americans in the media. He points to the cultural narratives that have bamboozled us into believing stereotypes and other cultural concoctions that limit and diminish African Americans in multiple ways. By choosing this title, I aim to offer another way to access understanding about how cultural narratives get constructed and the power they have to dismiss and make invisible "Others." And even though Lee is talking about black people in the media and I am talking about black people and the environment, there is a common thread where power and privilege by design can diminish our ability to see people's historical and contemporary experiences more fully and in relation to our own experiences. Bringing together cultural studies (in particular, popular culture), critical race theory, and environment allows me to create a framework that is expansive and flexible enough to engage the complexities and contradictions of the African American environmental relationship. That complexity—layered, messy, informed by power dynamics (who gets to produce, disseminate, and represent information)—reveals the need to draw on diverse sources of material to begin to address the nuances and richness of a relationship that is not necessarily served by a linear distillation using traditional frameworks. As mentioned earlier, I also engage and value popular material and other knowledge gleaned from nonacademic sources in the exact same way that I engage scholarship. This is particularly true concerning knowledge about, by, and for African Americans, because historically, African Americans have not always had access to traditional spaces of learning and knowledge production and have used other sites of production, such as music, art, and popular culture to have their/our voices heard. As Bernice Johnson Reagan, scholar and founding member of the singing group Sweet Honey and the Rock said in a keynote speech on black

BLACK FACES,
WHITE SPACES

Introduction

Surely i am able to write poems
celebrating grass and how the blue
in the sky can flow green or red
and the waters lean against the
chesapeake shore like a familiar,
poems about nature and landscape
surely but whenever i begin
"the trees wave their knotted branches
and . . ." why
is there under that poem always
an other poem?

—From *Mercy* by Lucille Clifton

n May 2006, *Vanity Fair*, a monthly magazine with national distribution, published a special issue focusing on environmental issues. Labeled the "Green Issue," it had such celebrities as Julia Roberts and George Clooney, resplendent in green, alongside politicians Al Gore and Robert F. Kennedy Jr., gracing its cover. Inside the issue, Al Gore outlined the global warming "crisis" and then shared the "good news" that "we can solve this crisis, and as we finally do accept the truth of our situation and turn to boldly face down the danger that is stalking us, we will find that it is also bringing us an unprecedented opportunity" (Gore 2006, 171). Following his optimistic proclamation were twenty-eight pages of photos and text reflecting the voices of well-known eco-activists, environmental organizations, and celebrities who are considered proactive in combating the world's environmental crisis. Among the sixty-three pictures and profiles, however, only two pictures of African Americans (and one African, Nobel Peace Prize winner Wangari Maathai) could be found.

It might be tempting to dismiss this striking imbalance because of the issue's celebrity-driven feel (even if Gore lent some gravitas). For a gossip-driven, advertisement-heavy magazine, allocating an entire issue to environmental concerns could also be construed as a bold move. But there was nothing groundbreaking about who the magazine decided was the face of the environmental movement and who was seemingly at the center of the environmental debates. Sadly, although the environmental movement's expressed desire is to engage a broad and diverse constituency, this special issue reinforced for its thousands of readers that neither environmentalists nor media executives seem to recognize the significant role of race in the movement and its aims. In light of Hurricane Katrina (2005), where the complex interaction of race and environment have been highlighted in the media, scholars and practitioners were presented with an "unprecedented opportunity," as Gore put it, to address the connections linking race, identity, representation, history, and the environment—an opportunity to awaken from our "historical amnesia" and begin to create a more inclusive, expansive environmental movement devoid of denial and rich in possibility.

Vanity Fair's "oversight" in highlighting hardly any African Americans or other people of color in their "Green Issue" speaks volumes about how Americans think, see, and talk about the "environment" in the United States. The representation of environmental issues and the narrative supporting the visual images provides insight into *who* Americans think actually cares about and actively participates in environmental concerns. In addition, how the environmental narrative is portrayed will be an indicator of who is actually being engaged in the larger conversation.

If popular media is one effective way in which to transfer, inform, reinforce, and legitimate ideas about the environment (Braun 2003; Bloom 1993), *Vanity Fair* is not alone in creating a racialized perception that when it comes to concern for the great outdoors, participation in outdoor recreation in our forests and parks, and the environmental movement in general, African Americans and other nondominant groups are on the outside looking in. Other magazines such as *National Geographic* and its subsidiaries, *Outside*, and *Backpacker*, continue the tradition, lending authenticity to "original" stories of the American wilderness as fundamental American truth through photographic and discursive representations of the "Other"—other places and peoples (Bloom 1993). This racialization feeds stereotypes and ideologies that become entrenched in our national psyche (Elder, Wolch, and Emel 1998), and it can lead to forms of exclusion from places (housing, employment, etc.) and processes (educational opportunity, professional advancement) that are thought to be inclusive and reflective of the cultural and social diversity of the United States (Sibley

1995). A "white wilderness" is socially constructed and grounded in race, class, gender, and cultural ideologies (DeLuca and Demo 2001). Whiteness, as a way of knowing, becomes *the* way of understanding our environment, and through representation and rhetoric, becomes part of our educational systems, our institutions, and our personal beliefs (Sundberg 2002; DeLuca and Demo 2001; Smedley 1993).

Racialization and representation are not passive processes; they also have the power to determine who actually participates in environment-related activities and who does not; which voices are heard in environmental debates and which voices are not. The power of representation lies in its ability to shape today's reality through the reality of the past (Duveen and Moscovici 2001). Along with visual images, textual representation—the stories we tell about ourselves, others, and the places we live—"provides a framework for experiencing the material world" and for understanding "how local stories intersect with larger social, historical, and political processes" (Cruikshank 1998, xii).

Stories, or narratives, about our "natural environment" work in much the same way, informing our environmental interactions and shaping the institutions concerned with environmental issues (thereby shaping how we represent, perceive, and construct the identities of racial "others" within our society). The dominant environmental narrative in the United States is primarily constructed and informed by white, Western European, or Euro-American, voices (DeLuca and Demo 2001; Jacoby 1997; Taylor 1997). This narrative not only shapes the way the natural environment is represented, constructed, and perceived in our everyday lives, but informs our national identity as well. Missing from the narrative is an African American perspective, a nonessentialized black environmental identity that is grounded in the legacy of African American experiences in the United States, mediated by privilege (both intellectual and material, influenced by race, gender, class, and other aspects of difference that can determine one's ability to access spaces of power and decision making), and informed by resistance to and/or acceptance of the dominant narrative.

This book argues from the assumption that environmentalism and the meanings we attribute to the environment are grounded in history, race, gender, and culture. Let me clarify what I mean by "environmentalism" and other related terms. More than any other term, I use the words "environment" and "outdoors" interchangeably throughout this book. In addition, "wilderness," "parks," and "forests" are also employed to describe particular outdoor spaces. While each word has more specific meanings, these meanings also overlap. Many of the texts cited use the terms interchangeably. And notably, most of the people I interviewed used the terms interchangeably, too. This suggests that, for African Americans, specificity may be less important than the implied meaning underneath and that these terms have come to mean one and the same thing for the black community. Therefore, I use the term "environment" in this book to describe any outdoor green space, whether natural or constructed, insofar as it relates to environmental issues such as air quality, climate change, and species protection. "Environmentalism" connotes an activity or practice related to the outdoors, especially having to do with addressing a problem or a set of issues.

While the dominant mainstream culture has played a significant role in constraining (and making invisible) African Americans' engagement with environmental concerns and participation in environmental and nature "activities," there are also other perceived obstacles that need to be acknowledged. For African Americans, to varying degrees, the everyday practices associated with environmental interactions are directly related to issues of African American identity and American history (Dominy 1997). This ideology can be at odds with thinking about and honoring the environment in the way that the dominant narrative of conservation and preservation is constructed (Agyeman 1989). On the other hand, this way of thinking does not preclude a desire to care for, enjoy, and utilize the environment in a sustainable fashion. The ideas, thoughts, and solutions that arise from an African American experience of the environment are mediated by differential access, needs, privilege, and history.[1] They are no less valuable, visionary, or controversial. Some feel that if African Americans reclaimed their past they would "acquire a sense of agency to shape dominant narratives" (Finley 2001, 3). But others argue that economic disparity and limited access to resources keep African Americans from being able to express their environmental views and attitudes, thereby influencing how the environment is constituted and understood in the United States (Johnson et al. 1997; Bullard 1995). Other explanations for the perceived lack of responses to environmental issues have been apathy, disengagement, and/or fear (Blum 2002; Virden and Walker 1999; Grandison 1996; Smith 1996).[2] These responses are further complicated by "resistance" to ideas seen as "white," in an effort to construct a black identity (hooks 1992).

Representations and racialization inform the way we approach the "business," the "science," and the "conservation" of the natural world.[3] They affect the way these spaces and places are constructed and the institutions that maintain these constructions. By excluding the African American environmental experience (implicitly or explicitly), corporate, academic, and environmental institutions legitimate the invisibility of the African American in the Great Outdoors and in all spaces that inform, shape, and control the way we know and interact with the environment in the United States.

We can broaden our understanding of African Americans and environment interactions by exploring how the attitudes and perceptions of African Americans are influenced by racialized constructions and representations, informing how African Americans participate in the use of national forests and parks as well as other open spaces. While there is a growing interest on the part of some environmental institutions to understand and support greater participation by African Americans in natural resource management, I have found few empirical studies that specifically address African American attitudes in relation to environmental issues in the United States.

My goal in this book is to draw together key concepts and frameworks from several theoretical perspectives in order to understand and explain the intersections of racialization, representation, identity, and their subsequent impacts on African American environment relationships. I draw on frameworks from feminist geography, environmental history, and work on race and identity to examine these themes. In particular, I use feminist theories of identity, positionality, and relationality to highlight the mutual construction of place, identity, and subjectivity (Collins 2000; Nagar 1998; Pulido 1997; Friedman 1995; Haraway 1991). Where we are situated in our lives informs the narratives that we construct about our place and who we are in relation to self and others (Staeheli and Martin 2000; Haraway 1991). Such a framework takes into consideration how contemporary constructions of black identity are informed by "shifting class positionality" and can provide insight into how the African American identity is negotiated (individually and collectively) in the production of an environmental narrative in the United States (hooks 1994b, 147).

I also draw on environmental history methods to show how ideas of the environment have been constructed, disseminated, commodified, and understood in the United States over time. As a geographer, I find particular value in the work of historians such as Donald Worster (1990) and Carolyn Merchant (1990), who have worked to reveal the ways that people attribute meaning to the environment based on their ideologies, beliefs, myths, and experiences. By placing ideas of wilderness in a historical context and deconstructing their implicit and explicit racial connotations, scholars can push mainstream environmental institutions and the society at large to consider alternate understandings and experiences of the outdoors (De-Luca and Demo 2001). By investigating the shifting "cognitive maps" of the spaces we think of as the "natural environment," we have an opportunity to rethink how African Americans in the United States have engaged those spaces.

In addition to feminist geography and environmental history frameworks, exploring race and identity provides insight into the linkages between identity and representation. I focus particularly on the ways in which media and formal education promote certain ways of knowing, explaining, and understanding over others. Whoever has representational authority can determine how our stories get told and how we think about ourselves in relation to others (Behar 1995; hooks 1992). Theorists investigating race, and in particular, the construction of an African American identity, suggest that we interrogate the forms, themes, and regimes of representation in order to problematize and politicize the representation process (Hall 1996). Stories can shape self-understanding; for African Americans, theorization of black culture within an environmental context can illuminate historical elements that inform environmental interactions today (Dyson 1999). For that reason, this book not only critiques the historical absence of African Americans from mainstream environmental narratives, it also focuses on foregrounding the narratives of African Americans who have shown leadership, creativity, and commitment to engaging environmental concerns within and in relation to their communities.

Finally, in an effort to build a bridge between cultural studies, critical race studies, and environmental studies, I have expanded my conceptual framework to include representations of the black experience found in cultural productions such as art, music, poetry, and literature. While more traditional or formal theories of knowing can provide powerful information supported by accepted methods of research and analysis, cultural sites that express alternative ways of knowing and seeing the world offer an opportunity to "draw outside the lines" of the traditional frameworks, which don't always capture the nuance of lived experience of nondominant cultural groups, such as African Americans. In constructing a narrative or story about African Americans' environmental relationships, these forms of creative expression not only reveal the many ways that African Americans are "having fun, getting serious, establishing credibility and consensus, securing identity, negotiating survival, keeping hope alive, suffering and celebrating" (Wideman 2001, xx). They also give credence to practices and cultural spaces that are often devalued or dismissed in more formal sites of knowledge production.

What are some of the issues arising from the "African American experience" in the United States that inform the attitudes and beliefs African Americans hold about the environment? Academics have explored various questions related to people, nature, and representation (textual and visual). Scholarly work on representation has highlighted how power, personal interests, and unchallenged historical accounts of the past influence how places and peoples are represented (Day 1999; Duncan 1993). In addition, geographers have addressed issues of exclusion, marginality, and space, particularly how images of groups and places can combine to create "landscapes of exclusion" (Agyeman and Spooner 1997; Cloke and Little 1997; Sibley 1995). In particular, Sibley discusses how "key sites of nationalistic sentiment" such as the countryside implicitly excluded black people (Sibley 1995, 108). Investigation of racial discourse within geography has explored the mutual constitution of race, space, and place, the construction of the Other, and the power of racialization processes to shape environmental interactions (Kosek 2006; Braun 2003; Gilmore 2002; Pulido 2002; Sundberg 2002; Wilson 2000; Day 1999; Nast 1999; Gilbert 1998; Jackson 1998; Woods 1998; Kobayashi and Peake 1994; Radcliff and Westwood 1993; Anderson 1988). More recently, a number of books have explored the relationship between race and food (Alkon and Agyeman 2011; Guthman 2011). However while geographers are exploring new frontiers with work on race, there has been a reduction in research on African Americans themselves (Mitchell and Smith 1999; Dwyer 1997). Some have charged that there has to be "social relevancy" for a subject to be pursued. Others contend that if race is "central to the contemporary human condition," then race is central to geography (Shein 2002, 1). I have undertaken this research to expand the conversation on race and environment broadly by highlighting the experiences, perceptions, and beliefs of African Americans as informed by history, memory, media representation, and dominant environmental narratives. In particular, by engaging cultural sites of production where African American knowledge continues to inform/define black identity and cultural practices in the United States, I want to change the way we think about African Americans in relation to all things environmental.

Within the field of environmental history in the United States, some scholars have begun to explore how race, class, and gender differences are significant to our understandings of ecological history (Glave and Stoll 2006; Krech 1999; White 1996; Anthony 1993; Worster 1993; Merchant 1989;

Nash 1982). The growing literature around environmental justice, with its particular focus on environmental racism and equity, has been one site of such work (Sze 2006; Cole and Foster 2001; Pulido 2000; Bryant 1995; Bullard 1995; Camacho 1998; Miller, Hallstein, and Quass 1996; Mohai 1992). While this literature highlights how African Americans and low-income communities are disproportionately exposed to environmental hazards, it also suggests that focus on environmental racism can lead to greater involvement in environmental issues by African Americans (Sheppard 1995).[4]

Other recent work on race and the environment includes an examination of "whiteness" and the challenges underlying assumptions about place, nature, and race (Smith 2007; Moore, Kosek, and Pandian 2003; Braun 2003; Sundberg 2002; Bonnet 2000; DeLuca 1999). For example, Braun (2003) explores the absence of the African American adventurer in popular media and how this is apparent in representations of risk-taking in the natural environment. Encounters with nature in publications that address outdoor sports are portrayed differently depending on whether the magazines target middle-class white readers or African American or Hispanic readers. In particular, when magazines targeting black or Hispanic readers portray activities in the outdoors, the focus is largely on recreational sports or relaxation, not adventure or risk-taking (Braun 2003).

In the leisure/outdoor recreation literature, a number of studies highlight the degree of participation by African Americans in certain open-air activities (Holland 2002; Johnson et al. 1997; Roberts and Drogin 1996; Philipp 1995; Sheppard 1995; Baugh 1991; Agyeman 1989). Empirical studies have found that African Americans are less likely than Anglo-Americans to visit outdoor recreation areas or participate in recreation there (Johnson et al. 1997; Sheppard 1995). Reasons cited include socioeconomic factors, such as education and income, and subcultural values informed by discrimination, slavery, and African heritage (Johnson et al. 1997; Meeker 1984). Scholars addressing environmental attitudes of African Americans have found that compared with Whites, African Americans are fearful of forest environments because of threats from wildlife and other humans (Virden and Walker 1999). In particular, researchers have suggested that racism plays a significant role in limiting black participation with the "Great Outdoors." For example, Patrick West (1993) describes how in the 1970s, a city park in Chicago had signs that read "whites only; niggers keep out." Dorceta Taylor describes how African Americans prior to World War II were attacked when visiting recreation areas designated as "white" (Taylor 1989). Travel to and from recreation sites has also been cited as a barrier to African American since they may fear to travel through unfamiliar, sometimes remote terrain considered white and hostile (West 1993). Still others suggest that because African Americans today are largely an urban population "removed from the land," they may be less affected by the negative images of the forests and other wildlands that plagued their ancestors (Johnson et al. 1997, 75). Finally, studies have challenged the perception that African Americans are not concerned with environmental issues (Mohai 2003; Baugh 1991). A study in 2001 that queried African American parents in Texas, while acknowledging that a history of slavery may influence black attitudes toward nature, revealed a heightened awareness of environmental issues as a result of direct experience (pollution and sewage) and a belief that environmental education was important for their children (Kahn 2001). Additional studies have explored the role of race and class in American environmentalism, highlighting how mainstream environmental agendas marginalize and exclude people of color (Taylor 1997). Most of the studies fall short in systematically investigating the impact of visual and textual representations, attitudes and beliefs, and collective memories on African Americans interactions with the environment. General accounts of African Americans' experiences in wild lands and other green spaces are usually personal narratives found in travel literature, race and identity literature, or memoirs rather than comparative, quantitative, empirical accounts (Deming and Savoy 2011; Griffen and Fish 1998; McElroy 1997; White 1996; Harris 1988). While not providing social scientific or fully documented data, they do present important insights for considering how African Americans negotiate collective memories of their underrepresented history in relation to an environmental narrative that largely denies or marginalizes their experience.[5]

Furthermore, the lack of comprehensive studies addressing the nature of a black environmental imaginary in the present hinders our understanding of how African American environmental interactions have developed and changed over time (Blum 2002). We know little about the meanings African Americans attribute to the natural environment (Virden and Walker 1999; Johnson et al. 1997).[6] It is not enough to "recapture the spirit of the past" (some romantic ideal of people's historical relationship with the environment) to assure ecological respect in the present (Runte 1997, xxii). Our efforts to engender respect and inspire active participation in the care and management of our forests and parks means embracing the cultural experiences and environmental values of all segments of American society.

Those in representation-making positions of power keep reproducing the same statements and ideas. At the same time, African Americans are weighed down by a conflicted environmental history and a contemporary environmental experience that appears to ignore them (Kahn 2001; Meeker 1984).[7] Both processes contribute, in varying degrees, to perpetuating the myth of an environmental narrative in the United States that is all-inclusive, meaning the same thing to all peoples, despite historical and cultural differences that inform people's experiences. (I explore this topic further in Chapter 1.)

RESEARCH QUESTIONS, METHODOLOGY, AND SITES

In order to broaden our understanding, I began this research with the following overarching question: What are the linkages between representations of the "Great Outdoors" and the "African American experience" in the United States, in terms of the attitudes, beliefs, and interactions pertaining to the environment? I wanted to understand the relationship between African Americans and various processes that define and inform what we call "environment" (whether as matters of discourse or aspects of the natural world). Since there are many dimensions to this question, I specifically look at four areas that I address in detail in the following chapters.

First, I look at the role of collective memory of race-relations in the United States and how this "memory" informs environmental interactions. For many African Americans, the ability to name, frame, and claim a green space is partly grounded in collective and individual memories that inform how they navigate and understand such spaces. Whether consisting of simply shared familial experiences or particular historical moments (like Jim Crow), memories prove to be powerful incentives in determining the characteristics of an African American's relationship to the environment.

Second, I wanted to explore how representations of the Great Outdoors are racialized within environmental institutions and organizations. As mentioned before, representations of the Great Outdoors can intentionally or unintentionally feed stereotypes of who is engaged with the environment and who is not. A narrative is constructed about the environment that is deemed at once authentic and universal and that denies the complexity of experiences that nondominant groups have encountered historically. This in turn inhibits the ability of environmental organizations to develop opportunities and practices that recognize, attract, and support African Americans participating in environmental activities.

Related to this issue, I also want to understand how the relationship of African Americans to the environment is affected by representations and perceptions in the context of work, leisure, literature, education, and activism. Images, words, and stories about the African American environmental relationship have powerful roots in a history that has not always been kind or fair when considering African Americans as citizens capable of participating in the nation-building process. These negative stereotypes, often grounded in racist practices from our past, have bled into present-day narratives (e.g., Hurricane Katrina) perpetuating old grievances and creating new roadblocks to a more expansive consideration of African American contributions to our ongoing environmental challenges.

Finally, I needed to take a closer look at how African American participation is perceived by environmental organizations as well as consider how African Americans actually experience the natural environment and the organizations that manage it. Even within the same environmental organization there can be a disparity in the perceptions of white staff and their African American colleagues. This disparity can lead to frustration, anger, and general fatigue on the part of all parties and inhibit their ability to collectively address underlying issues related to race and develop the capacity within the organization to work with diverse constituencies.

While these issues formed the basis of my original research, further reading and reflection enticed me to expand my original framework and questions to include cultural studies and black "voicings" from multiple sites, not as pawns and proxies, but for important insight into the depth of complexity that exists in the African American environmental relationship. Along with addressing the issues noted above, I also explore how popular culture and other sites of informal knowledge production change the way in which we understand that relationship. In a way, this is an attempt on my part to read between the lines of a history and a present that does not always recognize or acknowledge other ways of seeing and encountering the world. In addition, film, art, music, poetry, and literature created and produced by African Americans tell us something about the African American environmental relationship in the first person, so to speak.

What is potentially revealed by allowing African Americans to more fully express perspectives, visions, and understandings of their collective and individual relationship to the environment uncensored by accepted dominant narratives, definitions and representations of who they are? I believe we get a glimpse of something beyond the fear, contestation, and invisibility that can be part of the African American experience. We begin to see how, despite the challenges, resilience can emerge on the landscape and within our communities, revealing new practices of environmental engagement.

My research methodology and the research sites I spent time in followed a unique pathway. My choice of research design, that is, how to do it "rightly," was reflective of both my skills and my politics and as such, calls for transparency and explanation. But first I want to talk a bit about my primary research site.

My primary research was conducted in Miami-Dade and Broward Counties, which have proximity to the Everglades National Park, Biscayne National Park, and Big Cypress National Preserve in southern Florida. The region known as "South Florida" was chosen for specific reasons. In 1934, the Everglades National Park became the first major park without mountains and waterfalls to become committed to total preservation (Runte 1997). Today, intense pressure from residential development and agricultural needs threatens to destroy this unique wetland environment. Some charge that it is the most endangered park within the national park system (Boucher 1991). As a result, numerous constituencies in southern Florida have made it their task to restore the health of the Everglades while striking a balance between the needs of that environment and the needs of local people (Douglas 1997). In addition, both Biscayne National Park and Big Cypress National Preserve are steeped in histories that include African American interaction with the land (farming and logging) that has informed present-day environmental practices. Southern Florida is also home to one of the most ethnically diverse spots in the United States. African Americans have "consistently formed an important and sizeable component of the South Florida population" (Mohl 1991, 112). Race relations in this southern state have always been a visible and sensitive issue (Mohl 1991).

Southern Florida is rich in African American history that is directly related to environmental activities. For example, Virginia Key Beach, the only beach in Miami during the 1940s where African Americans could go, has recently been restored. In Biscayne National Park, rangers discovered that Parson Jones, a black man born in the 1800s, had owned three of the islands in the park. His family had 250 acres where they farmed, fished, and went sponging.[8] In addition, a network of local, state, and national organizations is directly concerned with increasing African American user participation in environmental issues related to national parks and forests in the area. Along with Earthwise Productions, these organizations include the South Florida Ecosystem Restoration Council, which focuses on educating communities of color and getting them involved in the Everglades Restoration, the Virginia Key Beach Trust, and the South Florida African-American Leadership Council organized by the director of community outreach for Audubon, South Florida.

Once ensconced in South Florida, I used multiple approaches to get at the issues I've outlined earlier in this chapter. I did this because, at the core, I want to understand three main things: (1) how African American participation is perceived by environmental organizations; (2) how African Americans actually experience the natural environment; and (3) what insights we can gain into the organizations that manage these environments. Each of these points are informed by the ideas outlined in this chapter and will be explored in more detail throughout the book: dominant narratives, history and memory, media representation, race and racism, and resilience. Since these are complex issues that overlap each other, I employed different methods that would ultimately allow me greater insight into the linkages between African American identity, attitudes, and values, representation and environmental interactions with forests and parks, and the natural environment more generally in the United States.

Data collection involved five specific activities that addressed the three primary issues noted above. I wanted to get a sense of how African Americans in the environment are portrayed in popular outdoor magazines and other media materials. So I used something called Content Analysis where I examined particular magazines and brochures with an environmental bent and literally counted how many times we see African Americas and in what context they are pictured (see Chapter 4).

I also interviewed African Americans from all around the nation, many with specialized environmental knowledge related to forest and park activities, as well as others who may or may not access or use forests and parks. I traveled to, or met with individuals from, the District of Columbia and many states, including California, New Mexico, Alabama, Missouri, Pennsylvania, Colorado, Washington, and Florida.

Along these same lines, I provided surveys to white staff at three national parks in South Florida. Taken together, the interviews and surveys allowed me to document the values and motivations of an emerging constituency of African Americans involved in forest and park use. In addition, I could begin to track the perceptions of those working for the National Park Service (NPS) to get a sense of where the realities experienced by black and white park staff were different.

But I also wanted to understand more than what I could glean from the answers that everyone gave me in the interviews and surveys. So I used

Participatory Research, and Participant Observation, two techniques that allowed me to access multiple layers of experience not always observed when using conventional data-collection methods. Basically, I found other opportunities outside of the interviewing process that provided additional insight into the issues I was exploring. These ranged from an impromptu content analysis of the popular media coverage of the August 2005 Hurricane Katrina and its aftermath,[9] which occurred during the analysis and writing of my research, to my observations of discussions, individuals' behavior, and even confrontations in the context of conferences and workshops that I attended. My immersion in the everyday life of the Miami-Dade County area for one year also provided a rich source and constant stream of encounters and observations related to African Americans and the environment and to the material and representational landscapes of my study area.[10]

KEEPING IT REAL

As an African American doing research on race in the United States, I was mostly seen as an insider. For the majority of the study participants, my race "membership" was enough to establish trust and to share with me their thoughts on race and the environment. Other studies have shown a positive correlation between black informants' comfort level in sharing sensitive thoughts on race and the interview being conducted by another African American, the implication being that having black skin in common creates a space of trust (Twine 2000). But in other cases, particularly when I tried to establish relationships with African Americans who were not park and forest users, it was different. For example, accessing black churches proved nearly impossible for me. I am not a member of any church, and while some African Americans I spoke with belonged to churches, they were hesitant to introduce me to their congregation. While I was temporarily living in the community, I was still only a visitor—a stranger. Having no formal relationship with such an important institution as the church in this community hindered my ability to interview a broader constituency. In addition, in some of my less-structured conversations with African Americans, I felt there was some suspicion about whether black people who lived in that community could trust those who did not. For instance, would the information they might share with me be used to further my purposes, but not necessarily theirs?[11]

Additionally, as a black researcher specifically addressing issues on race, I struggle against any pretension to "represent my race." As a professor of

African American history at Harvard, Henry Louis Gates Jr. discusses this dilemma in his work—balancing the competing demands of doing research using his acknowledged skills, methods, and explanatory frameworks and simultaneously satisfying the "dreaded requirement to represent" his race as a black person in the United States—something Gates finds himself continuingly struggling against (Klotman and Cutler 1999, xxii).

Finally, it has been important for me to explicitly situate myself in this work on black experience with the environment in order to avoid any romanticizing or exoticizing of "the Other." Instead, particularly when presenting this work at conferences and workshops, I attempt to highlight the "communal values and subjectivities" of us all (Klotman and Cutler 1999, xix). Also, as a scholar, I focus on providing support for "traditionally ignored or discredited sources of what might be called black voicings" and converting "such implicit declarations of freedom into disciplinary capital" (Klotman and Cutler 1999, 214).

But there is also something else. It would be disingenuous of me to ignore that I am part of a small, but growing cadre of African American scholars who are actively researching the nexus of race and environment from a variety of perspectives. While this work continues to influence the way we think about and participate in environmental issues, the larger environmental debate has been historically dominated by Euro-American voices. What does it mean for me to write about the environment, not only as a scholar or a geographer, but as a black woman, born and raised in a nation where difference, and specifically race, informs relationships, shapes debates, determines access, and constitutes meaning? Toni Morrison, in her book *What Moves at the Margins*, puts it this way:

> For me—a writer in the last quarter of the twentieth-century, not much more than a hundred years after Emancipation, a writer who is black and a woman—the exercise is different. My job becomes how to rip that veil drawn over "proceedings too terrible to relate." The exercise is also critical for any person who is black, or who belongs to any marginalized category, for historically, we are seldom invited to participate in the discourse even when we were its topic. (2008, 70)

Writing this book is an opportunity for me, paraphrasing black feminist scholar Patricia Hill Collins, to reclaim black *people's* subjugated knowledge while intentionally declaring my own standpoint as the place to begin this work (Collins 2000, 13). In her book *Black Feminist Thought*, now in its second edition, Collins talks about the "exclusion of Black women's ideas from mainstream academic discourse" and challenges the idea that there is such a thing as a scholar/activist dichotomy (12). So here I stand—situated, positioned, transparent (and yes, a little defiant)—in hopes that I can offer something Morrison calls "a gesture towards possibility" (2008, 70–71): That we recognize that the differences we bring to any discussion about the environment can only expand what we know and how we choose to stand in relation to each other. And that what becomes "possible" in our efforts to create and sustain the human-environment relationship is continually replenished by the diversity of ideas that is the domain of all of us.

CHAPTER OUTLINE

I begin this exploration by situating the environmental experience of African Americans in relation to the dominant narrative about the environment in order to consider the linkages between how the Great Outdoors is represented and the "African American experience" in the United States. In Chapter 1, entitled "Bamboozled," I start by examining the challenge of relying on a one-size-fits-all narrative that marginalizes or makes invisible the environmental experiences of nonwhite peoples on the American landscape. Using film references and Patricia Limerick's argument that more complex narratives might involve a more diverse public, I consider the legacy of an environmental narrative that denies the complex history of various cultural groups whose access to and use of natural resources were mediated by policies and laws that limited their possibilities. What are the cultural artifacts that are left over from the implementation of "master narratives" that obscure more complex and dynamic interactions between African Americans and the environment? In the section entitled "Black Faces, White Spaces," I review the history of African American engagement with the mainstream environmental movement from the early 1900s to the present (including the National Park Service, the Forest Service, and the environmental justice movement). I also take a closer look at the creation of national parks and forests as spaces and places that reflect national identity, environmental values, and American history that are not immune to processes of representation and racialization. By referencing the work of classic environmental history scholars such as Alfred Runte, Donald Worster, and Carolyn Merchant along with insights from Dorceta Taylor, Paul Mohai, and Kevin DeLuca we can begin to see how the environmental experiences of African Americans have been marginalized, whitewashed, or simply left out of the dominant narrative. More important, we begin to understand the challenges that mainstream environmental organizations like the National Park Service face when actively trying to build relationships of reciprocity with diverse communities across the United States. What results is that African Americans are at the back of the proverbial bus in terms of being visible and instrumental in developing strategies within mainstream environmental circles to deal with environmental change. Yet individual and collective efforts by some African Americans challenge traditional approaches, policies, and assumptions about African Americans and create new opportunities to expand our existing environmental narratives in order to address contemporary environmental issues.

But before we can begin to consider some of those responses/approaches/new ideas, we will delve a little deeper into the roots of that American story, exposing the linkages to Eurocentrism, the individual perspectives of a privileged few (e.g., John Muir), and the historical need for natural and cultural resource protection. In Chapter 2, entitled "Jungle Fever" (with another nod to Spike Lee), I explore the history of how the environment has been constructed in the United States (academically, politically and through organizations) and popular culture, highlighting how African Americans have been constructed in relation to nature. Specifically, I start off with an analysis of the 2010 *Vogue* cover shot of basketball star LeBron James and supermodel Gisele Bündchen that illustrates how African Americans have been negatively depicted in relationship to nature while reinforcing the idea that the environment is a "white" space and a white concern. I examine the historical trajectory of conceptualizations of African Americans and their relation to nature, such as their being called "savage," "wild," or the "missing link"; conceptualizations that have bumped up against Euro-American ideas of nature that have taken precedence in the collective American environmental imaginary, mediated by federal agencies, legislation, and mainstream environmental organizations. The work of Donna Haraway and Paul Outka reminds us that African Americans have historically undergone repeated cultural interrogations regarding their status as humans within the larger society. The legacy of these cultural constructions reveals a thinly veiled contempt for black people that continues to be expressed in intellectual, political, and cultural sites (as evidenced by the *Vogue* cover shot of LeBron James). This historical and contemporary denigration of African Americans explains some of the reticence on the part of African Americans to participate in mainstream environmentalism. The analysis looks at how black people were marginalized in the ongoing nation-building project during the nineteenth and twentieth centuries.

While processes at the national scale conspired to keep African Americans on the sidelines in the dominant conversation about American identity, this does not mean that African Americans did not construct their own set of stories and understandings about the environment. By drawing on experience and memory, both collective and individual, African Americans used their own set of knowledge to inform their relationship to the environment. In Chapter 3, "Forty Acres and a Mule," I consider the ways in which African Americans have negotiated dominant environmental narratives by inserting their stories into the mix. David Delaney uses "geographies of experience" to signify how life experiences are connected to spatial organization. For African Americans, constructing geographies of experience demands a drawing on of both collective and individual memories, many of which are indicative of a painful and contested American history. These memories, particularly those collective memories that are linked to key historical moments such as slavery and Jim Crow segregation, can have significant impact on African American environmental interactions in the present. So I lay out my argument detailing the connection between environment, memory, and race and how this relationship influences African American participation in environmental management. In particular, I discuss key historical periods of African American history with a specific focus on slavery and Jim Crow segregation and how these moments shaped African American connections to place. Using data I've collected, particularly interviews with African Americans actively engaged in environmental work, I explore the many ways that collective memory expresses itself either in the preservation of African American history in a designated park or historical site (such as Cane River Creole National Park in Louisiana or American Beach on Amelia Island, Florida) or in the ways it can restrain or motivate individual agency and participation in environmental activities, such as forest and park management and use. Ultimately, I conclude that memory, both collective and individual, plays a key role in shaping African American attitudes about the environment primarily because of the connection between personal memory and a collective history that has defined the black experience as one of struggle, exclusion, and pain, particularly in relation to place.

While history plays a significant role in understanding the African American experience in relation to the environment in the United States, our contemporary practices concerning the way African Americans are represented in the media and in educational circles also informs present-day environmental interactions. In Chapter 4, entitled "Black Faces," I explore more closely how the paucity of visual and textual representation of African Americans in popular media, the National Parks, and environmental education perpetuates the invisibility of African Americans in conversations about environmental management. Using Hurricane Katrina as an entry point into the conversation, I examine the power representational processes that have set into place stereotypes and viewpoints about African Americans in the present that continue to impact African American environmental participation and identity. Representation effectively shapes those perceptions and beliefs at multiple scales, both public and personal. Specifically, I review background literature and provide the conceptual frameworks I employ on black identity and representation (tapping into the work of Michael Eric Dyson, Cornel West, Manning Marable, and bell hooks), highlighting representation as a key site of struggle for African Americans. What follows is a brief look at the history of black representation in the popular media, including television, magazines, and film (with a particular focus on *Outside* magazine). I examine the National Park Service with an eye toward exploring how African Americans have been represented in park brochures and interpretive exhibits. In addition, I present evidence that African American concerns and interests in relation to the environment have not been articulated, invited, or understood by the context of the mainstream environmental movement and natural resource management. Finally, I address the ways black identity is narrowly defined or poorly articulated and often results in limited interest and participation by African Americans in work projects having to do with the environment.

This brings us to the ongoing debates within mainstream environmental organizations interested in attracting African American communities and individuals to their environmental work. In Chapter 5, "It's Not Easy Being Green," I discuss racism and diversity, two hot-button topics that people seem to embrace or reject, but which arise either implicitly or explicitly in the "environment" conversation.[12] Many environmental organizations, while actively looking to diversify their staff and increase their involvement with diverse communities, are often hamstrung by rules and habits that keep them from fully understanding how racism, perceived or real, impacts African American participation. Furthermore, there are differences in the way many organizations perceive African Americans' participation in the natural world and the way African Americans actually experience the natural environment and the organizations that manage it. So I discuss the challenges that racism and diversity present to African Americans and mainstream environmental organizations that are interested in creating more inclusive contexts in which diverse individuals and communities can enter into environmental management. In addition, I discuss some of the primary debates on racism and diversity and present findings that highlight the frustrations and concerns of African American professionals and leaders who struggle to develop strategies that effectively deal with racism in practical ways within decision-making contexts. What is revealed is that there is a general disconnect between African American environmental professionals and their white counterparts regarding the perception of exclusion and racism within an environmental context. This lack of agreement and understanding of how race and racism have infiltrated our work and our lives continues to create roadblocks to building strong relationships between mainstream environmental organizations and African Americans.

But despite these roadblocks and the historical spaces that African Americans have had to contend with, African Americans have survived and thrived in the face of adversity. Zora Neale Hurston, in her book *The Sanctified Church*, honors the "unique spiritual character" of the southern black Christian church through folklore, legend, and popular mythology. Taking her lead, I consider the "sanctified" character of the black environmental experience in the United States that is also revealed in story, music, and history. In Chapter 6, "The Sanctified Church: How Sweet It Is," I consider the role of fear in shaping the environmental perspectives and practices of African Americans. In particular, I employ the work of Joy DeGruy Leary to examine how the legacy of oppression and violence against black people in forests and other greens spaces can translate into contemporary understandings that constrain African American environmental interactions. I also consider the role of resilience and agency by exploring some of the ways that African Americans are engaging "green" in their communities (i.e., the green economy) and the ways in which creativity is being leveraged by individuals and communities in service of livelihood needs. I then consider implications for our future—the consequences of engaging or *not* engaging a broader constituency in the climate change debate and the role of the "new" voices in the regeneration of our communities. Finally, I conclude this book by briefly reviewing the primary points of each chapter and offering ideas on how we might, depending on our interests, move forward. I invite the reader to consider the chapters as a series of layers that can be considered separately, but together create a "nested but not neat" scenario that, depending on your vantage point, reveals some of the contradictions and synergies of the African American environmental relationship.

CHAPTER ONE

Bamboozled

Perhaps his idea of ornament does not attempt to meet
conventional standards, but it satisfies the soul of its creator

—Zora Neale Hurston, *The Sanctified Church* (1981)

If it had been different in the beginning, it would be different now.

—Henry Finney, as told to author

W hile working on this book, I watched the movie *Far and Away*,
starring Tom Cruise as the son of a poor Irish farmer and Nicole Kidman as the daughter of a wealthy landowner, set in the
1800s. (I had seen it before.) It focuses on Europeans, both rich and poor,
who were driven to leave their homes in Europe and come to the United
States, seduced by the promise of land ownership. I was particularly in-
trigued by the lengths people would go to claim and name land for themselves and their families. At one point in the film, when Cruise's character
realizes that he may never own land if he stays in Ireland, he remembers
his father's dying words: "land is a man's very own soul," which in his mind,
justified any action he might take to claim land for himself. The movie cul-
minates in a sweeping depiction of the race for land under the Homestead
Act of 1862 that saw thousands of European Americans risk injury and even
death in order to stake their claim on the most desirable parcels of land in
the West. Considered to be one of the most important pieces of legislation
in American history, the Homestead Act, captured in this cinematic moment, highlights the European American struggle and desire to own land,
a particular way of thinking that embedded in our psyches the "truth" that
land (and more specifically land ownership) is directly connected to what it
means to be an American.

But there are some holes in this story. This piece of history does not
exist in a vacuum. While I allowed myself to be swept up in the very human

experience of survival in a new frontier, I also thought about the Trail of Tears (1838–39) when the forced removal and relocation of thousands of Native American peoples also resulted in injury and death. In 1830, when many of the characters portrayed in *Far and Away* were still standing on European soil, Congress passed the Indian Removal Act, which authorized the removal of Indians from their lands and the implementation of reservation policies that reduced the size of their traditional lands. Consequently, Indian tribes left the Ohio and Mississippi valley, many unwillingly, and headed west. Approximately 17,000 Cherokees walked from Georgia to Oklahoma in what came to be known as "The Trail of Tears."[1] They lost their homes, their livelihoods, and in many cases their lives.

At the same time as the characters in *Far and Away* began to consider the overseas voyage to the North American continent, Hispanos (this term specifically identifies people of colonial Spanish descent who live in the Southwest) in New Mexico were struggling to hold on to their land grants protected by the Treaty of Guadalupe Hidalgo (1848). This peace treaty between the United States and Mexico was supposed to transfer ownership of 525,000 square miles of land (including parts of present-day Arizona, California, New Mexico, Texas, Colorado, Nevada, and Utah) to the United States in exchange for $15 million (equivalent to well over $300 million in today's dollars).[2] In addition, and most importantly for these descendants of Spanish settlers, Mexicans and Metizos, the treaty was supposed to ensure the safety of preexisting property rights of Mexican citizens in the transferred territories (DuBuys 1985).

Instead of guaranteeing the right of Hispanos to have land on which to live, grow, and thrive, the treaty allowed them to be systematically disenfranchised of their land.[3] This process of disenfranchisement included undercutting some land grants, such as Las Trampas in New Mexico, a community land grant where equal portions of land were given to each farmer and his family (similar to the distribution of land to families under the Homestead Act). But, like many promises that the United States failed to honor, the people of the village of Las Trampas lost their one useful economic resource and were now landless, living in an amazingly rich landscape that was no longer theirs (approximately twenty-one thousand acres of the Las Trampas land grant are now in possession of Carson National Forest). To this day, New Mexicans are using legal channels to reclaim this land, their history, and their lives (Lucero 2009).

At another point in the film, Cruise's character is employed by a railroad company to lay tracks in the Ozarks. I think about the Chinese laborers who were primarily responsible for building the railroads that made it possible for people to travel west, build settlements, and thrive in a hostile landscape. (I imagine many of the characters in *Far and Away* would rely on the railway for goods and transportation.) Ironically, although there are plenty of historical records highlighting that by the summer of 1868, approximately two-thirds of the four thousand workers who built the transcontinental railroad over the Sierra Nevada and the Great Plains were Chinese, the Central Pacific Railroad tried to cheat them out of this history by writing them out of the narrative of constructing the rail line. The railroad excluded the Chinese from ceremonies and even from the famous picture of the golden spike—the last one—being driven into the road bed, symbolizing its completion. Despite the monotony of the job, the contempt and systematic abuse incurred, and the lower pay received despite the longer hours demanded of them (while having to pay their own board), the Chinese laborers continued working until the railroad was completed (Chang 2004). Adding insult to injury, the Central Pacific laid most of them off and did not even pay for their passage back home, which had been promised. Consequently many of the Chinese were homeless and jobless in an unfriendly environment, without the protections and opportunities afforded many of the European American characters in *Far and Away*.

Finally, I can't help but consider my own ancestors, enslaved Africans recently freed from the chains that bound them, given land to call their own only to have it taken away before the seeds of their new beginning could grow (more on this in Chapter 2). These free men and women were denied participation in the land grab under the Homestead Act by the United States government, and the ripples of that decision are imprinted on our psyches and in our present-day economic, social, and political relationships.

There are many stories on the periphery of American history, a history that gains traction in the American consciousness and becomes a kind of default narrative illustrating what we believe is the best of who we are collectively and tells the "truth" of how we got here. While there is no denying that certain moments in history, like the implementation of the Homestead Act, had a sweeping impact on the way humans engaged with the natural environment, for many this narrative as it is traditionally told is a broad stroke that obscures the difference of experience and possibility, which are mediated by political, cultural, and economic forces. How does the past illuminate our understanding of the present as it relates to environmental engagement?

In *Mission to Environmentalists*, Patricia Limerick challenges present-day environmentalists to eschew the narratives that lack complexity and use "historical knowledge" to better understand "contemporary environmental politics" (2000, 171). While certain narratives offer us an arguably more palatable history, Limerick warns us that a linear and simplistic story can give the impression that all Americans have a shared understanding and agree about how people should interact with nature.[4] Limerick puts it this way: "Broadening the environmental movement to include the great diversity of the national population requires a full reckoning with this history" (184). Ongoing conflicts between various cultural groups and federal, state, and local environmental organizations often point to historical tensions related to the use, access, and naming of particular natural resources such as forests, water, and land. Whether it is a tribe fighting for the right to maintain the sacredness of Devil's Tower in Wyoming, the organization known as Las Trampas in New Mexico seeking to reclaim land once owned by their ancestors, or the reparations movement seeking redress for the thousands of acres of land unfairly removed from black hands, present-day environmental engagement reveals a historical lineage that not only tells us something about various nondominant cultural groups, but also challenges notions that a single narrative can be all things to all people. More important, when we consider contemporary strategies to engage nonwhite people in the mainstream environmental movement, we limit both our understanding and ability to build meaningful relationships by premising our action on stories that only address one perspective or experience. We are at risk of drawing flawed conclusions that do not consider the legacy of a past that provided a different starting point for particular cultural groups. A more comprehensive understanding of the past can be useful to understanding different groups' motivations, perceptions, and challenges to environmental engagement in the present.

At the end of *Far and Away*, amid the chaos of wagons, horses, and people, Cruise's character finally claims a piece of land that he can call his own. While this interpretation of the Homestead Act is arguably a fairly accurate representation of some people's experience (i.e., European Americans), the story as told in *Far and Away* avoids the nooks and crannies of American history that expose whole worlds of experience that run counter to the preferred narrative of environmental encounters that appear to be an equal opportunity domain for all. We can be duped into wishful thinking that our common past shares the same characters and circumstances producing similar outcomes, making it easier to ignore the tensions in which we presently stand.

In this chapter, I consider the legacy of an environmental narrative that denies the complex history of various cultural groups whose access to and use of natural resources were mediated by policies and laws that limited their possibilities. In particular, I explore the impact this legacy has had on the participation of African Americans with the mainstream environmental movement from the early 1900s to the present (including the National Park Service, the Forest Service, and the environmental justice movement). I pay particular attention to the creation of national parks and forests, as spaces and places that reflect national identity, environmental values, and American history and that are not immune to processes of representation and racialization. Finally, I consider how African Americans are challenged in terms of being visible and instrumental in developing strategies within mainstream environmental circles to deal with environmental change.

BLACK FACES, WHITE SPACES

Historically, African Americans have not been well represented in the major environmental organizations in the United States (Mohai 2003). In the early 1900s, the "environmental movement" had its first public demonstration over the conflict surrounding the proposed dam to be built on the Toulumne River, also known as Hetch Hetchy, in northern California (Taylor 1997). The controversy drew well-known environmentalists such as John Muir and the Sierra Club and "thrust environmental issues onto the public stage" (31). Suddenly, regular people felt they had a say in public debates about different environmental issues. But for the most part, these citizens were white and middle class, and the environmental groups that were formed during this time period were largely segregated by race and class (31). This would remain a central characteristic of environmental organizations as they grew in number over time. According to a study of 1,053 environmental organizations (listed in the 1992 *Gale Environmental Sourcebook* and the 1993 and 1994 *Conservation Directory*), there were 78 new organizations by 1913 and 214 organizations by 1959. In the post–Rachel Carson era of the 1970s "membership in eight major environmental organizations [including the Sierra Club, the Wilderness Society, and the Audubon Society] increased from 892,100 to 1.583 million" (Taylor 1997, 41). But a number of studies revealed that membership was largely white. In 1969, a survey of Sierra Club members showed that most were white and middle class. In addition, a 1975 study that focused on environmental volunteers found that 98 percent of the volunteers were white as well (40).

The mainstream environmental movement did not seem to increase its diversity much in the 1980s and 1990s, and environmentalism continued to be defined from a white, middle-class perspective.[5] One result of the increasing homogenization of the participants and the agenda was the birth of the environmental justice movement, which challenged the mainstream environmental movement to look at the way race shapes environmental experiences and practices (Taylor 1997). In 1990, nine activists of color wrote a letter to what was called the "Group of 10"—the major environmental organizations in the United States—requesting, among other things, that these groups employ more people of color in their organizations. At the Second National People of Color Environmental Leadership Summit in 2002, environmental justice leaders and mainstream environmental representatives agreed that there had been little progress in increasing ethnic and racial diversity on the staff and boards of the mainstream environmental organizations since that letter was written.[6]

Along with environmental organizations, environmental participation in outdoor recreation appears to have primarily a "white" face. There have been a number of national studies over the last twenty years that have addressed African American participation in outdoor recreation areas (Floyd 1999). The 1985–87 Public Area Recreation Visitor Study by Hartmann and Overdevest (which included the U.S. Forest Service and the National Park Service) showed that 94 percent of visitors were white and 2 percent were African American. In particular, African Americans "exhibited the lowest rate of participation in backpacking, camping both in developed and primitive areas, wildlife observation and photography, canoeing and kayaking" (Floyd 1999, 7). Another study commissioned by the U.S. Department of the Interior in 1996 found that African Americans participated in fishing, hunting, and wildlife viewing much less often than whites.[7] For instance, only 2 percent of African Americans engaged in wildlife viewing, compared to 13 percent of European Americans (8).

Studies of the National Park Service (NPS) have shown that there is a lack of diversity both in park visitation and park hiring practices. In the NPS Comprehensive Survey of the American Public on racial and ethnic diversity, the findings revealed that while 36 percent of white respondents reported visiting a national park within the last two years, only 13 percent of African Americans visited any of the parks within the same period. African Americans had the lowest rate of visitorship among all study participants, which included Native Americans, Asians, and Hispanics (Solop, Hagen, and Ostergren 2003, 1). In terms of employment, African Americans do not seem to fare much better. In her book *National Parks and the Women's Voice: A History*, Polly Welts Kaufman speaks about the challenges facing women and minorities who work in the national park system (Kaufman 1996). A 1995 study showed that more than half of the NPS employees (53.5 percent) were white males, while about one-third were women; minorities accounted for about 20 percent of the employees (239). The Forest Service does not fare much better. In 2002, there were only about 1,300 African Americans working in the Forest Service, out of approximately 44,000 employees (Hendricks 2006, 4).

Along with a lack of visible African American participation in mainstream environmental activities, visual representations of wildlands and other green spaces remain largely focused on a Euro-American experience of the environment. According to Derek Martin, who undertook a study of media images in mainstream magazines, there is a "racialized outdoor leisure identity" that views outdoor enthusiasts as generally strong, young, and white (2004, 514). While earlier studies have shown that African Americans were underrepresented in magazine advertisements in general, there has been some improvement. *Time* magazine showed an increase in their use of black models from 1.3 percent in the 1950s to 14.9 percent in the 1990s. But Martin found "no studies that examined differences in the geographical settings that models occupy" (2004, 519).[8] In the three magazines he reviewed over a five-year period (*Time*, *Outside*, and *Ebony*), the majority of advertisements featuring people outdoors used white models. Martin suggests that there may be a linkage between low levels of participation in outdoor recreation by African Americans and the racialized outdoor leisure identity perpetuated by the popular media, and he advocates for further research.

Dominant narratives and existing representations provide the context from which environmental organizations and African Americans draw their cues about how to think about the environment and themselves. Both groups absorb, integrate, and create meanings (often expressed by political, academic, cultural, and popular voices) that are attached to each process, which informs the practices of diverse environmental organizations and various groups of African Americans.

While I am primarily concerned with taking a broad view of African American participation in all things environmental, a part of this research focuses specifically on the National Park Service. Focusing on an environmental institution that lays claim to representing an American identity that is an integral part of the wilderness areas that it seeks to protect allowed me to observe at a micro scale how the larger macro scale influences of representation and narrative influenced their environmental practices, specifically as it relates to African American participation. Again, national parks and forests, as spaces and places that reflect national identity, environmental values, and American history are not immune to processes of representation and racialization. In particular, national parks and forests can unintentionally become sites where African Americans experience insecurity, exclusion, and fear born out of historical precedent, collective memory, and contemporary concerns.[9]

What is the "American" story about the Great Outdoors? American conceptions of the natural environment have shifted over time, influenced by social and political processes, reflecting ideas about culture and nation (Spence 1999; Elder, Wolch, and Emel 1998; Nash 1982; Oelschlaeger 1991). From the mid-1800s through the 1930s, the acceptance of wild landscapes inhabited by natives peoples as being natural evolved into an idealization of uninhabited landscapes representing national identity and requiring preservation (Spence 1999). Scientific professionals, such as George Perkins Marsh and individual enthusiasts like Henry David Thoreau and John Muir, championed these ideals that are still the bedrock of American environmental ideology today (Taylor 1997).

The narrative of the Great Outdoors in the United States is explicitly informed by a rhetoric of wilderness conquest, Romanticism, Transcendentalism, and the belief that humans can either control or destroy Nature with technology (Lowenthal 2000; Virden and Walker 1999; Taylor 1997; Worster 1993; Nash 1982). Implicitly, it is informed by a legacy of Eurocentrism and the linkage of wilderness to whiteness, wherein both become naturalized and universalized (DeLuca and Demo 2001; Agyeman and Spooner 1997). Prominent views of nature, while not unified, draw from the experiences of those in a position to influence and establish legitimacy for their ideas institutionally and culturally. Furthermore, these narratives, which contribute to the American environmental imaginary, are grounded in the values, beliefs, and attitudes of the individuals who construct them. These attitudes and beliefs manifest in our everyday environmental practices, affecting our livelihoods and our interactions with each other.

For example, the environmental views of John Muir can be found in his contribution to the creation of six national parks, in the tenets of the Sierra Club, and in popular outdoor and adventure magazines today (Oelschlaeger 1991, 172). Muir's perspective on the natural environment, while influenced by other readings of the wilderness (Thoreau) was also informed by values of whiteness and his religious beliefs (DeLuca and Demo 2001; Worster 1993).[10] This is most reflected in his effort to portray Yosemite as a sacred place to be saved from civilization by comparing American wilderness to Europe's cathedrals and regaling the white man's god (DeLuca and Demo 2001).

John Muir had very specific views about African Americans that reflected insensitivity to certain people. On his "Thousand Mile Walk to the Gulf" in 1867 through lands that had been devastated by war, he spoke of Negroes as largely lazy and easy-going and unable to pick as much cotton as a white man. While his environmental ethic included wilderness, it clearly did not include nonwhites (Merchant 2003). "Before we sanctify Muir, we need to understand how his racial attitudes affected his commitments to conservation" (Gelobter et al. 2005, 8).

The national park system is a site where cultural identity, environmental values, and American history intersect and are actively transmitted to the public. The reiteration of these ideals is reflected in park policy, in historical interpretive programs, and in the way national parks and forests are represented in popular media (Lovett 1998). National Parks were originally created out of the belief that the natural "wonders" of the United States should be preserved for present and future generations (Runte 1997). In time, the purpose of the parks was expanded to include conservation concerns and cultural resource protection (Lovett 1998; Dilsaver 1994). These ideas emerged out of the desire of nationalists to distinguish the United States from Europe, and the experiences of a privileged few who had access to the intellectual and physical spaces where the national park vision was created (Runte 1997). But the growth of the national park ideal did not take place in a historical vacuum. Throughout American history, diverse cultural values and beliefs, race relations, and material needs have informed, implicitly or explicitly, the nature of the park system. Consequently, some charge that minority and ethnic groups do not share the values associated with the national parks that the National Park Service emphasizes (Meeker 1984). Previous studies have shown that among different racial and ethnic groups, African Americans are less likely to participate in recreation activities than whites (Vale 1995). While economic limitations have been cited as primary reasons why nonwhite peoples, and in particular, African Americans, lack enthusiasm for the national parks, others feel that a history of subjugation to the land and racial prejudice have given rise to general indifference to national park concerns (Meeker 1984).

A number of programs within the NPS have addressed diversity issues. But responses to these various efforts from those working with the park service and those outside the park service are not all favorable. At some parks, there is a tension between the desire to attract African American interests through interpretive programs and the park's primary focus on protecting the natural resource. Others resist diversity programs designed to increase the African American presence in management and other positions.

Among the more successful programs initiated by the National Parks Conservation Association (NPCA) were the Mosaic in Motion conferences. A follow-up report to the Mosaic in Motion conference in 1999 addressed the real and perceived barriers that keep people of color from seeing the national parks as belonging to them as well as the rest of the nation. It also addressed the need for greater interpretation of race and ethnic history in national parks and diversification of the national parks workforce (U.S. Department of the Interior 2002).

More recently, the Second Century National Parks Commission and the NPS Advisory Board have been focused on the issue of relevancy.[11] In particular, the NPS is eager to build relationships of reciprocity with diverse communities across the United States. Through initiatives designed to increase the cultural competency of the NPS while identifying opportunities to build new relationships with surrounding communities, the NPS has made "relevancy" one the four priority areas to focus on as it approaches its centennial in 2016. The NPS recognizes that there are "substantial differences between the demographics of the United States population and the makeup of the NPS workforce, visitors to national parks, and participants in NPS and partner programs." By intentionally working on creating learning opportunities for communities and park service staff, the NPS believes it can play a significant role in addressing "such varied societal challenges as declining historical and cultural literacy, climate change, and reconnecting Americans—especially youth—to nature" (Finney and Fraser 2011, 1).

BACK OF THE BUS

When I was growing up, I remember my parents and other proud black people providing examples of smart, risk-taking, bold women and men who had contributed to American life and culture. How many black children like me heard about agronomist George Washington Carver, educator Mary McLeod Bethune, and explorer Mathew Henson? How often had I had a book by a black author thrust into my hands that provided a viewpoint on the world—a *story*—that my parents hoped would sow seeds of pride and belief in my right to be here and an awareness of what I had to contribute? For many African Americans, this surge in making visible what was invisible was a direct response to a historical narrative and contemporary processes that tried to diminish, devalue, and erase black experience, creativity, and the possibility to positively influence the *human* experience. We were at the back of the bus, metaphorically and literally, when considering our participation in a democratic society that prided itself on innovative thinking and bold initiatives that inform the American way of life.

When thinking about the mainstream environmental movement in the United States, I began to wonder if we are not once again, at the back of the proverbial green bus. In this chapter, I have attempted to highlight the limitations of an environmental narrative that does not consider the historical lineage of pain and prejudice experienced by African Americans. The manifestations of these omissions inform contemporary policies and practices, sometimes resulting in incremental shifts in mainstream environmental organizational praxes or instead, the creation of separate movements and/or actions by nondominant groups to address the needs of the African American community. While there are clearly African American individuals who are making their "green" mark—attorney and activist Van Jones, MacArthur "genius" winners Will Allen and Majora Carter, and planet walker John Francis—they represent only the tip of the iceberg of African American thinkers and doers who, day in and day out, are rethinking green and recovering and redefining what it means to be in a healthy relationship with the natural environment. With a nod to Rosa Parks (who became a literal and symbolic expression of our right and our need to be seen as human beings who are able and willing to claim their rightful place as full citizens), it is time to make our move once more. Consider the changing demographic face of America, the impacts of climate change and a human/environment relationship that is experiencing growing pains like no other time in history. There is little room for business-as-usual antics or organizational action plans that allow themselves to be hijacked by "tradition" and limited vision. Instead, it is incumbent on all of us to rigorously recognize, consider, and support new ideas, experiences and configurations of human/environment interactions. For African Americans, "by any means necessary" takes on a whole new meaning.[12]

CHAPTER TWO

Jungle Fever

What form does love of nature take in a particular historical context?
For whom and at what cost?

—Donna Haraway, *Primate Visions: Gender, Race and Nature
in the World of Modern Science*

White folks sure know how to make some nice foliage.

—from Aaron McGruder's comic strip, *The Boondocks*, April 24, 2005

A picture speaks a thousand words. In the case of the April 2008 cover of *Vogue* magazine featuring famous sports figure LeBron James and supermodel Gisele Bündchen, a picture can also generate controversy, frustration, and charges of racial insensitivity (Sullivan 2008).[1] The image of six-foot, nine-inch James, the first black man to grace the cover of *Vogue*, with a menacing grimace on his face and in an aggressive stance while lightly holding the fair-haired Ms. Bündchen, bore an uncanny resemblance to a 1917 recruitment poster featuring a menacing gorilla holding a white woman that reads "Destroy This Mad Brute—Enlist" (Figure 2).

In February of 2008, the *New York Post* published a cartoon by Sean Delonas that appeared to compare the first black president to a "rabid" chimpanzee. In a racially provocative response to the recently signed stimulus bill, Delonas depicted two white policemen, one with his gun drawn, standing over a fatally wounded chimp he had just shot, while the other says, "They'll have to find someone else to write the next stimulus bill." Some people felt that the cartoon was just highlighting how ridiculous the bill was (it was so bad, even a monkey could have written it), but others felt that it reflected a deep-seated set of views about race, violence, and primates that is insidious within the collective American consciousness (Stein 2009).

Figure 2. "Destroy This Mad Brute." H. R. Hopps, 1917.

Images can leave an indelible mark in our memories. For African Americans, the past and present are littered with representations that aggravate our collective sense of self as Americans and as human beings. When one considers that racial identity is not experienced separately from other facets of lived experience, the architecture of the African American environmental relationship begins to come into full relief. Teasing apart the strands of that story, we see not only the historical particularity of being black in America (segregation, slavery); we also see the entanglement with the white experience of nature that passes as universal and normative.

In her book *Primate Visions*, Donna Haraway reminds us that, in "European, American and Japanese societies, monkeys and apes have been subjected to sustained, culturally specific interrogations of what it means to be 'almost human'" (1989, 27). Since the "founding" of the New World by Columbus, African Americans have also undergone culturally specific interrogations of what it means to be not quite human. And the visceral response to the image of LeBron James in a menacing stance and the likening of President Obama to a dead chimp strikes a chord in the racial memory of a group of people who have worked hard to erase that nontruth from the narrative of their lives.

What has been the historical trajectory of how conceptualizations of African Americans and nature have bumped up against Euro-American ideas of nature that have taken precedence in the collective U.S. environmental imaginary? How has this relationship been mediated by federal agencies, legislation, and mainstream environmental organizations that continue to define collective people/environment interactions in the United States?

My aim in this chapter is not to undermine efforts to explicitly address the human/environment relationship; instead, I wish to challenge the universality that denies the differences in our collective experiences of nature in the United States, thereby limiting our ability to understand how our unhealthy relationships with the natural environment are intimately linked to our unhealthy relationships with each other.

In addition, I am not attempting to draw a historical timeline of the black and white environmental experience in the United States. There are scholars who have done this and have done it well.[2] Instead, in this chapter, I examine how key moments in U.S. history that in many ways have come to define human/environment interaction in the United States bump up against collective experiences of black people navigating the social, cultural, and psychological minefields of slavery and segregation. In particular, how did the founding of parks, creation of conservation, and the broader environmental movement impact African Americans? What is the emotional and psychological "trickle down" effect of the way in which these moments/ideas impacted black people over the long term? How do we challenge, to paraphrase Haraway, a nature that seems innocent of *black* history? (1989, 156).

BIRTH OF A NATION, THE REMIX

I had the opportunity to visit the Charles H. Wright Museum of African American History in Detroit, Michigan. Along with temporary exhibitions, the museum boasts the world's largest permanent exhibition of African American culture, entitled "And Still We Rise."[3] Filling twenty-two thousand square feet, this exhibit "allows patrons to cross over time and geographic boundaries" in order to experience the collective African American journey from the beginnings of the slave trade in Africa to present-day life in the United States.[4] While the exhibit highlights significant moments in American history, what I found most powerful was walking through the part of the exhibit that was shaped like the upper and lower decks of an actual slave ship. On the upper deck, you see images and life-size reproductions of white slave traders and black slaves; the whipping and branding of black men and women by white men was presented as commonplace. Below deck, there are scores of life-size brown bodies squeezed in like sardines on shelves. When you emerge from this part of the exhibit, you see enslaved Africans being sold on the auction block and working the fields. In this depiction of the African American experience, this is the first visual experience that we have of black people relating to the natural environment in the United States.

This version of events is pretty standard within American history books as the cultural narrative that best represents the "first" black environmental experience on American soil: black people as slaves to a white master, working someone else's land for free. This account is in contrast to the narrative of the "environmental" experience of many European immigrants, who settled on the East Coast or crossed the Great Plains to grab their first piece of land under the Homestead Act of 1862. This is not to say that European immigrants did not have difficult experiences—setting up house and working the land could be dangerous, backbreaking, and isolating work. But there is a world of difference between working and living on your own land versus working and living as chattel on land owned by someone else, under the threat of the lash.

In the creation of a human/environment narrative that is particular to the American experience, both of these stories occupy a privileged position within our collective understanding of our past. Few would challenge the veracity of these events as stated or dismiss either narrative as being less than integral to the evolution of the United States as a nation and as an identity to claim. However, here are two points that I want to make. First, these racialized experiences of the natural environment were systematically mediated by institutions, legislation, and the social mores and beliefs of the dominant culture. Second, even though these two significant parts of American history were happening simultaneously, scholars rarely talk about, analyze, or consider the relationship between these two events in equal measure or the legacy of this relationship as it informs contemporary human/environment practices and beliefs (with some notable exceptions like Kimberly Smith, Paul Outka, and Kevin DeLuca). Specifically, I argue that it is the relationship between these two events, not just the singular event of slavery, that sets off a trajectory of "black" experience and "white" experience, that would come to define natural resource practices for African Americans in very specific ways. It also illustrates the relationship between access to resources, power, and wealth and the capacity of history and memory to define environmental management practices for a particular group. (I examine this last point more closely in Chapter 3.)

There are other key players in this story, including American Indians, Chinese, and Mexican immigrants. For the purpose of this chapter, the scope of my argument will be limited to addressing the black and white environmental experience through the lens of environmental management/legislation, land ownership, and the emergence of conservation and preservation as ideological cornerstones in the United States. I recognize the limitations of a story that does not include all the key players, or appears to compartmentalize the experiences of various groups. But my intent in this chapter is to highlight the *relationship* between specific events and their subsequent influence on the development of an African American environmental imaginary.

During the latter half of the nineteenth century and the beginning of the twentieth, a number of significant thinkers, pieces of legislation, and events emerged that greatly influenced environmental practices, ideologies, and the positions of different groups of people in relation to the manifestation of these influences on the landscape. In the 1860s, slavery was abolished and westward expansion was in full force; black and white alike were drunk with the possibility of land ownership. The Emancipation Proclamation and the Homestead Act would initially allow approximately forty thousand freedmen to receive four hundred thousand acres of abandoned Confederate land and two million European immigrants to lay claim to 160-acre parcels of land, respectively. The infrastructures were put into place to manage these processes. Congress established the Freedmen's Bureau in 1865, and one of its many functions was to supervise and manage all abandoned and confiscated land in the South and to assign tracts of land to former slaves.[5] In the case of the parceling out of hundreds of acres of land to thousands of individuals and families under the Homestead Act, the United States government instituted specific rules that all claimants had to meet in order to claim and retain ownership of their parcel of land. This is where any broad similarity in the fervor over land acquisition in the two stories ends. Both the South and the West possessed culturally specific challenges, especially as it relates to the political and social makeup of both landscapes. In the South, the former white owners of the land, who were pardoned after the war, began to pressure President Andrew Johnson to allow their land to be returned to them. They were afraid that black landowners and farmers would start to accumulate wealth and power in the South. On February 5, 1866, in response to their request, Congress defeated that portion of the Freedmen's Bureau Act that gave it the authority to assign land to former slaves, and President Johnson ordered all land titles rescinded. The freedmen were forced off their newly acquired land, and it was returned to the former white plantation owners. In an effort to secure land for freedmen, many proposals were presented to the president and Congress. One proposal suggested providing transportation for freedmen out west where they could acquire land under the Homestead Act, just like European immigrants. But President Johnson vetoed every proposal that provided land to former slaves.

As black men and women responded to and regrouped from the emotional whiplash of events that they were experiencing, John Muir would give his first lecture on forest preservation around 1875, revering the "pristine-ness" of nature. Over the next twenty years, Muir would be influential in the creation of Yosemite as a national park and the founding of the Sierra Club, now the oldest and largest environmental organization in the United States. During the 1880s, Gifford Pinchot began thinking about a career in forestry, and in 1898, approximately thirty years after the Emancipation Proclamation, became known as the "father of conservation" (that is, the rational planning and efficient use of natural resources), and would become the fourth chief of the Division of Forestry. While the two men would eventually part ways as friends because of ideological differences, an environmental juggernaut had been launched using rhetoric and logic that resonated with powerful constituencies, including the president of the United States. Both men had the ear of President Theodore Roosevelt, who sanctioned the creation of the National Park Service and the Forest Service, and their ideas about forests and park management and use continue to inform how we talk about and interact with the natural environment today.

While Pinchot and Muir explored, articulated, and disseminated conservation and preservation ideologies, legislation was being enacted to limit both movement and accessibility for African Americans, as well as American Indians, Chinese, and other nonwhite peoples in the United States. This included the California Land Claims Act of 1851, the Black Codes (1861–65), the Dawes Act (1887), and the Curtis Act (1898). During the same period, there were numerous race-related massacres of African Americans: two hundred in Louisiana in 1868; nine in North Carolina in 1898; and seventy in Colfax, Louisiana, in 1873 (Myers 2005).

How do we reconcile the proactive, expansive, and innovative ways in which Pinchot, Muir, and Roosevelt committed themselves to working with forests and land resources with the knowledge that thousands of freed black men and women could not, even under the Homestead Act, gain access to or ownership of these resources? And where any attempt to challenge the status quo could lead to violence against African Americans, which at best was ignored or overlooked, and at worst, was condoned and accepted?

In his work *Race and Nature: From Transcendentalism to the Harlem Renaissance*, Paul Outka (2008) provides some insight into how these two radically different historical moments can be understood in relation to one another. Outka forces us to examine the relationship between the "profoundly entangled—and bitterly divisive—constructions of nature and race in the United States" (2). He calls attention to the "legacy of making people of color signify the natural" as a prelude to exploitation of nonwhite peoples and the natural environment:

> This legacy—in which whites viewed black people as part of the natural world, and then proceeded to treat them with the same mixture of contempt, false reverence, and real exploitation that also marks American environmental history—inevitably makes the possibility of an *uncomplicated* union with the natural world less readily available to African Americans than it has been to whites, who, by and large, have not suffered from such a history. (3)

Engaging in a kind of intellectual time travel, we can go back and forth between the contemporary image of a black man in an ape-like stance and the world of Muir and Pinchot and begin to see the roots of the disconnect, pain, and emotional residue that fuels the African American environmental imaginary. On the surface, the justification for limiting opportunities for African Americans at that time in history could be labeled economic or political. There have been numerous scholarly accounts about the economic and political motivations for slavery and segregation in the United States. In addition, scholar Kimberly Smith eloquently reminds us that when a people are denied their freedom, their relationship to the natural world is distorted and impaired (Smith 2007). But what lies beneath is more insidious: black people were seen as less than human, which precluded their being recognized, supported, and engaged with at the level that European Americans as a whole were accustomed to. This singular idea or belief was perpetuated in diverse arenas: "European culture for centuries questioned the humanity of peoples of color and assimilated them to the monkeys and apes in jokes, medicine, religious art, sexual beliefs and zoology" (Haraway 1989, 154). "For most of American history, statements about race were usually also statements about nature, about 'natural' racial differences, whether created by God or evolution" (Outka 2008, 6). The emerging narrative that defined "the Negro's place in Nature" managed to, in one fell swoop, place black people at the bottom of the evolutionary rung while reifying whiteness as closest to God, thereby morally justifying any act of exclusion from the nation-building project that was foremost in the minds of European Americans (Baker 1998, 14).

One strand of this emerging narrative was the eugenics movement. Defined as an effort to cleanse the human species of genetic defects and other "undesirable traits," eugenics informed Roosevelt's idea of a "new nationalism" that "placed the moral issue and patriotic duty of conservation into the context of a racial conversation" (Wohlforth 2010, 22). Many modern-day mainstream environmental organizations understandably disavow, dismiss, or even deny any connection to the tenets of eugenics that emphasize "purification" of the human gene pool by discouraging the reproduction of those with objectionable traits. But what cannot be erased is the involvement of key environmental proponents such as Roosevelt and Pinchot, in the development of an evolutionary understanding about who we are as human beings, the role race and nature play in the growth of the nation, and the determination of which human beings are privileged in that narrative. Academic institutions and museums such as the American Museum of Natural History and the Smithsonian guided and legitimated this process through research, rhetoric, and representation in exhibits and scholarly journals. It was the expositions in the United States—the world's fairs that took place in Philadelphia in 1876, New Orleans in 1885, and Chicago in 1893—that exposed a predominantly Euro-American public to images, words, and experiences that extolled a future where racial purification and the "richness of the country's natural resources" symbolized national power and possibility (Wohlforth 2010, 23). The place of whiteness in the racial hierarchy was amplified by exhibits and displays that diminished and distorted the lives and contributions of American Indians, Chinese, and other nonwhite peoples to the continued growth and development of America (Rydell 1984). "Blacks . . . were seen as examples of human nature, particularly of the child in man, and not as full human beings in their own right" (29). By saturating the "new citizenry" with racist propaganda disguised as a utopian dream, museum curators, anthropologists, and politicians effectively encouraged the continuing systematic brutalization of black people and fueled the growing chasm between the practice of stewardship of our natural resources (as defined by Roosevelt, Pinchot, and Muir) and the treatment of African Americans and other nonwhite peoples in the United States.

By seeking to cultivate a sense of national affiliation by appealing to what is arguably our deepest human fear—extinction—Roosevelt and others were able to justify an approach that allowed for African Americans and other nonwhite peoples to be systematically excluded, ignored, and erased (metaphorically and literally) from the larger conversation about who we are as a country. To believe that you can isolate one idea from another in the formation of a major movement in our country (in this case, the environmental movement) is to deny, first, the damage that has occurred, and second, the understanding that it is the pieces of a whole that have allowed certain actions and practices to be legitimized as a result. As Charles Wohlforth wrote in *Conservation and Eugenics: The Environmental Movement's Dirty Little Secret*, "The purpose failed, but the existence of the debate suggests the durability of the links between racism, nationalism and conservation" (2010, 27).

An important cultural vestige of this relationship is the promulgation of the narrative that black people and animals are in close proximity to each other on the evolutionary ladder. In the words of Elder, Wolch, and Emel (1998), "racialization of those with darker skin . . . feeds into entrenched ideologies, stereotypes and discursive practices, and demarcates the boundaries of national culture and belonging to place—and excludes those who do not fit" (185). But it becomes very hard to rid the collective consciousness of an idea that has grown roots in our institutions and cultural milieus, no matter how unsavory or how long ago the idea was originally planted.

There are numerous examples of how blackness and primitivism were constructed and disseminated in scientific, professional, and public venues during the nineteenth and early twentieth centuries. In particular, the most famous (and arguably the most egregious) case of dehumanization in pursuit of reinforcing white supremacy was that of Saartjie Baartman, the daughter of a Khoisan shepherd who was promoted, prodded, painted, and publicly debased in London between 1810 and 1815 (Ewen and Ewen 2008).[6] But here in the United States, Anglo-America was also keen on promoting an idea of racial superiority that could be the foundation of a strong national identity. Anthropologists, entrepreneurs, and museum curators embraced this task with fervor, exploiting Africans, Native Americans (including the Apache leader Geronimo), and other indigenous peoples in museums and world's fairs across the country.

The following story held the attention of the American public and provides an example of the depths to which some people would go to secure their position in an expanding nation. Ota Benga was a twenty-three-year-old Bushman from the Congo, living as a slave in Bashilele when he was "discovered" by Samuel Phillips Verner, an entrepreneur who had been commissioned to bring back pygmies to the United States. For a period of two years Ota Benga became a "traveling" exhibit: part of a larger road show where he was paraded as both spectacle and scientific "fact," reaffirming the inferiority of black peoples. In 1906, he was brought to the Museum of Natural History and became an "ethnographic display." But the powers that be decided that this venue would not provide the greatest opportunity for the paying public, so he was sold to the Bronx Zoo, and at the behest of the zoo's directors, he was housed in the primate exhibit, which proudly promoted Ota Benga as the evolutionary "missing link." While his stay at the Bronx Zoo was cut short due to widespread protests, many others thought that the ends justified the means. Ota Benga had become the poster boy for the "close affinity between African savages and their primate brethren," which further justified the need to retain and protect white purity (Baker 1998, 17). Within the larger narrative about the role of nature and culture in the construction and maintenance of a national identity worth preserving, black and brown peoples were seen as "interstitial, able to cross and bridge the distance between species with little effort" (Berenstein 1994, 316).

> For an Anglo-American population fearful of the massive influx of immigrants that was under way, and struggling to control a large free black population, the spectacle of a man living in the same cage with an orangutan offered tangible reassurance that the world was, in fact, inhabited by people of unequal worth. (Ewen and Ewen 2008, 136)

This belief, shored up by science, became part of the foundation from which America as a collective has continued to draw to assuage our fears and to justify the means dominant groups use to achieve their goals for "the good of us all." The collateral damage—the material, psychological, and physical impacts of these choices upon black and other nonwhite peoples in the United States is revealed and expressed in the strained relationships we have with each other and the tensions that exist in our human/environment interactions.

Flash forward to the image of LeBron James channeling King Kong, or the sound of Glenn Beck, conservative political commentator, likening Obama's America to a "planet of the apes" (*Huffington Post* 2010). These are not simply isolated incidences but reflections of what is embedded in our mental landscape about "visions of the primitive." According to Ewen and Ewen,

> Visions of human inequality that were popularized by scientists and showmen in two overlapping arenas, continue to occupy a place in visual popular amusements, most specifically in the practice of typecasting that continues as a routine in film, television, advertising, computer games, and perhaps of greatest concern, in the news of the day (2008, 139).

The notion was widely accepted among white people in the late nineteenth and early twentieth centuries that "black people are innately unfit for the responsibilities of citizenship; incapable of staying out of trouble, ignorant and uncultured; servile, scheming and brutish," (Ewen and Ewen 2008, xi). The American public today continues to be showered with images, words, and stories that sometimes explicitly, sometimes implicitly, intentionally or unintentionally, challenge the idea that an African American can truly represent the best of ourselves as a nation.

In their book *The New Countryside?: Ethnicity, Nation and Exclusion in Contemporary Rural Britain*, Sarah Neal and Julian Agyeman explore "how a particular space is seen and understood and experienced as *the* nation" (2006, 3). Who gets to participate in the nation-building project? What does that participation look like? Who gets to name and claim that space? By reconstructing nonwhite peoples as "Others" (in the case of Britain, "rural Others"), we relegate these communities to a marginalized position in which their "claims to rural space and national identity" may be denied (150). In the United States, this marginalization can render nonwhite people's economic, intellectual, and political contributions invisible within the larger process of nation-building, which makes the process of claiming national identity (and the rights and freedoms that come with that identification) much more challenging.

Going back as far as the world's fairs in the late 1800s and early 1900s, African Americans, American Indians, and Asians were misrepresented or neglected in the creation of the American exhibits that gave the world an opportunity to see what America as a nation was made of. In the 1876 world's fair in Philadelphia, many African Americans hoped to participate, "to demonstrate their contributions to America's historical development" (Rydell 1984, 27). But no matter whether it was Frederick Douglass, hoping to give a lecture to the crowd, or a committee of African American women providing both ideas and funds for the planning and construction of the exposition, or black artists looking to share their work, anyone who looked "black" was routinely ignored or denied the opportunity to participate on their own terms (Rydell 1984). While African Americans were barred from contributing to the larger narrative of American progress, what cannot be denied is the physical labor and mental ingenuity of African Americans, both those whose backbreaking work in the fields propelled the nation's economy forward, and those whose deep-seated belief in civic engagement changed our political and social landscapes.

Black artist Leonardo Drew illustrates the historical and human experience of nation-building in the United States in an art installation at the Corcoran Gallery in Washington, D.C.. As part of an art exhibit entitled "30 Americans," "Untitled #25" is an art piece made up of huge bales of cotton and wax that sits unobstructed and in your face in the middle of the room. The artist draws attention to human subjugation and how enslaved Africans helped build this nation, shape its economy, and transform the landscape. By using cotton in its most basic form, Drew points to the centrality of black people to the birth of this nation, rejecting any attempt to subvert the contributions of African Americans to the sidelines of American history.

In the mid-twentieth century, the United States reached its adolescence, so to speak, as a nation, and as such, we indulged our whims, stretched our limbs, and challenged anyone who got in our way. Consequently, by the late 1950s, we began to recognize the error of some of our ways and began to legislate values and behaviors that would set us straight as a nation, particularly as they pertained to race and the environment. The Wilderness Act and the Civil Rights Act are two of our most enduring and powerful pieces of legislation in the United States. Both legislative acts were passed in 1964, the Wilderness Act on September 3 and the Civil Rights Act on July 2. The power and longevity of these two documents are reflected in their influence on meaning, practice, and the elasticity of American identity. In particular, both pieces of legislation have influenced how we frame, name, and claim issues relating to environment and race. Their creation also provides some insight into the "disconnect" between the construction of race and of the environment in the United States and how this disconnect has manifested in the minds of Americans and the American environmental imaginary.

The Wilderness Act codified certain values put forth by environmental luminaries such as Aldo Leopold, David Brower, John Muir, and Howard Zahniser, namely the importance "for the continued existence of wild country in modern civilization" (Nash 1982, 200). These men believed in the historical significance of wilderness areas, the power of the wilderness to bring happiness and peace to human existence, and "the importance of maintaining a distinctive American national character" (225). The zeal with which these men pursued the wilderness ideal was matched by the amount of time and effort that Congress "lavished" on the wilderness bill, more "than any other measure in American conservation history" (222). Between 1956 and 1964, Zahniser, ensconced in what is now known as the Murie Center in Wyoming, wrote sixty-six drafts of the bill and steered it through eighteen hearings.

From 1945 until his death in 1964, Howard Zahniser, believed in the urgent need for a federal wilderness law. This became clear to him during the early 1950s, when the Wilderness Society was fighting the Interior Department's proposal to build two dams in Dinosaur National Monument in Colorado. His beliefs were buttressed by the ideas of John Muir, Henry David Thoreau, and Aldo Leopold and fueled his tenure as executive secretary of the Wilderness Society and editor of its magazine, the *Living Wilderness*. However there was some resistance, especially from oil, timber, mining, and grazing interests. In the end, Zahniser and his environmentalist brothers-in-arms had to cede some ground in order to see their bill signed, sealed, and delivered as law to the American people. Though Zahniser died a few months before President Lyndon Johnson signed the act into law in September of 1964, the work that he and other preservationists did to realize their environmental worldview as central to a healthy nation still reverberates in policy-making, academic, and public circles around the country.

While Zahniser worked on the multiple versions of what would become the Wilderness Act in Wyoming, an equally impassioned group of people with very different motivations convened at the Penn Center in St. Helena, South Carolina, to address the negative effects Jim Crow segregation had taken on African Americans, reflected in the loss of economic and emotional well-being and even loss of life. Black leaders, such as Dr. Martin Luther King Jr., Reverend Jesse Jackson, and Andrew Young of the Southern

Christian Leadership Conference (SCLC) began meeting with other members at the Penn Center. Even after the Civil Rights Act became law in 1964, from 1963 to 1967 members of the SCLC staff met at Penn Center every year for retreats, strategic planning, and training sessions to support and sustain the civil rights movement. Like the Wilderness Act, public support for the civil rights legislation came from various sectors, reflected in the participation of religious and labor groups and more than two hundred thousand people in the March on Washington for Jobs and Freedom in 1963. This event culminated in the delivery of the famous "I Have a Dream" speech by Dr. King on the steps of the Lincoln Memorial. For a nation still steeped in the vagaries of segregation and racism, the Civil Rights Act was a call to arms to uphold "the protections and privileges of personal power given to all people by law."[7]

While the language, tone, and relevancy of both these pieces of legislation were scrutinized in great detail, neither one was created in a vacuum. In the years prior to becoming law, both documents were directly or indirectly influenced by various incidents affecting the mood and manner of a nation struggling to define relationships between humans and the environment as well as between human beings. But the creation and manifestation of each document in relation to *each other* seemed to take place in discrete social, cultural, and geographical milieus. The only intentional confluence of events involving these two pieces of legislation seemed to be that they were both legislated/passed in 1964.

For the Wilderness Act, a number of key moments helped to set the tone, language, and tenor of this document. Though not meant to be an exhaustive list, we can begin to get a sense of what wilderness advocates were responding to and why:

1953 Between 170 and 260 people die in a smog incident in New York.

1954 On March 20, Supreme Court Justice William O. Douglas leads a "blister brigade" of hikers down the old Chesapeake and Ohio canal from Cumberland, Maryland, to Washington to oppose a highway that he believed would spoil the natural beauty of the canal. In 1971, the area became a 12,000-acre national park.

1959 Naturalist and conservationist George Schaller writes a book about mountain gorillas in the Congo entitled *The Year of the Gorilla* that would greatly influence the work of zoologist Dian Fossey.

1960 First Clean Water Act passes the U.S. Congress.

1960 Wallace Stegner writes "The Wilderness Letter" advocating federal protection of wilderness.

1961 President John. F. Kennedy tells the United Nations, "Every inhabitant of this planet must contemplate the day when this planet may no longer be habitable. The weapons of war must be abolished before they abolish us."

1963 Senate Subcommittee on Air and Water Pollution is created. Congress passes the Clean Air Act with $95 million appropriated for study and cleanup efforts at local, state, and federal levels.

For the Civil Rights Act, personal acts of defiance were coupled with collective responses to economic inequality and racism that many believed were destroying the very fabric of the nation:

1954 The Supreme Court unanimously agrees that segregation in public schools is unconstitutional in the landmark case *Brown v. Board of Education of Topeka, Kansas*.

1955 Emmett Till, a fourteen-year-old black youth from Chicago is visiting family in Mississippi when he is kidnapped, brutally beaten, shot, and dumped in the Tallahatchie River for allegedly whistling at a white woman.

1955 National Association for the Advancement of Colored People (NAACP) member Rosa Parks defies southern protocol by refusing to give up her seat at the front of the "colored section" of a bus to a white passenger.

1957 Formerly all-white Central High School in Little Rock, Arkansas, attempts to integrate nine black students, but they are blocked from entering the school on the orders of Governor Faubus.

1963 Martin Luther King writes "Letter from Birmingham Jail" in Alabama, where he is detained during antisegregation protests.

1963 Medgar Evers, field secretary for Mississippi's NAACP, is murdered outside his home in Jackson, Mississippi.

1963 A bomb is exploded at the Sixteenth Street Baptist Church in Birmingham, Alabama, killing four young African American girls who were attending Sunday school.

While both sets of historical events can be defined by their high emotional content and potential for violence and even death, there also seemed to be some inherent contradictions that neither piece of legislation dealt with directly. In particular, there are some underlying assumptions in the Wilderness Act that suggest its authors presumed a universality of ideals such as "the benefits of an enduring resource of wilderness" and "retaining its primeval character and influence" without considering the underlying structural and systemic inequalities that prohibited "all men" from participating in and actively enjoying the American wilderness, however it was defined. In particular, The law focuses on the use of wilderness areas for the public purposes of recreation, scenic viewing, scientific understanding, education, conservation, and historic preservation. But which public? Segregation was still an everyday part of American life. Even if the color of your skin or your gender didn't prohibit access, access was still limited even for those who could participate in public venues. (Additionally, there was limited information available—there were a few hearings and some published information in newspapers.) Some of the language adopted by Zahniser and others revealed a lack of awareness or sensitivity to the historical meanings embedded in certain words or phrases. For example, wilderness areas are described as "primitive," which carries with it some negative connotations, particularly for nonwhite peoples.

The creators of the Civil Rights Act were arguably better at addressing widespread systemic issues concerning every citizen's right to the "full and equal enjoyment of goods, services, facilities, privileges, advantages, and accommodations" by stopping "discrimination in public accommodation" and protecting the "constitutional rights in public facilities and public education." But there is no explicit discussion about the natural environment and the constitutional rights of the American public.

In both cases, arguments can be made for why each group of people needed to focus as they did on these separate pieces of legislation. Thoughtful individuals privileged what they thought was most important at that time. There were limited resources and energy requiring one to "choose one's battles." Some believed that the issues highlighted in each document didn't impact everyone equally; who really cares about hiking in the woods compared to getting a good job? If you were an educated, well-to-do white man in America, all doors seemed open to you—while you might agree on the need to fight for equal rights, that was someone else's fight. One can also argue that the positive attributes of both documents far outweigh their shortcomings. What is evident is the way in which these "separate but equal" documents were not in conversation with each other, but were instead created with a singularity of focus and purpose that only enhanced a false separation between humans and environment and to some extent delayed the moment when the tenets of each would need to confront each other and address that tension.

There's a saying that "nature always finds a way." That despite human beings best efforts to keep certain processes and phenomena separate, controlled, and managed, the messiness of life reminds us that we are simply part of a larger system. There is a little-known incident that took place in 1960 which I believe illustrates the danger inherent in keeping the subjects of these two documents separate. A white professor of theology from Boston University was planning an upcoming vacation at a National Park in Canada for himself, his wife, and an African American couple who were good friends. Aware of the hostilities toward black people in the United States, Dr. DeWolf wrote the owner of the Fundy Park Chalets in New Brunswick to eliminate any embarrassment that might befall his African American friends when they all showed up at the park. In his letter, Dr. DeWolf stated that he was "confident" that his friends would be treated well, but he just wanted to be sure. Dr. DeWolf described the husband as "university-trained, with four degrees, an author," and underscored that both the husband and wife were highly cultured people "of superior character." Dr. DeWolf did not get a response right away, and when he did, it was not the answer he hoped for. The owner of the chalets stated that because they get many American guests at their site, he could not "accept the possibility of embarrassment which may arise from this situation" (MacEachern 1995).

The irony of this story is that the African American couple that was refused a reservation at the Fundy Park Chalets in Fundy National Park was Dr. Martin Luther King Jr. and his wife, Coretta Scott King. Dr. King was simply exhausted from his civil rights work and wanted the chance to renew his spirit and focus on his writing. No doubt Zahniser, Leopold, Brower, and Muir would have understood Dr. King's impulse to choose a national park—a wilderness setting—to find that renewal, inspiration, and peace. But not even someone as distinguished as Dr. King, arguably the most visible icon of the civil rights movement, could escape the vagaries of that time, even by crossing the border.

CONCLUSION

In a talk at the University of California, Berkeley, William Cronon spoke about "a place where the past lingers." For African Americans, that "place" can be a present moment punctuated by symbols, stories, and images that are painful reminders of the reluctance of and resistance by the dominant culture to acknowledge black people on their own terms as full participants in matters pertaining to nationhood. A piece of cotton plucked from the land can reveal a painful past for some while only a distant memory for others. A tree in the woods can signify shade and spiritual oneness, and the end of a life so brutally taken. Or an image of a black man grimacing like a large primate can be humorous or degrading.

In this chapter I have taken a cue from Cronon (1996) to try to "understand the changing meaning and different cultural contexts that have characterized human life" by examining two different trajectories of environmental ideas and experiences in the United States and the impact the relationship between these trajectories has had on the African American environmental imaginary (35). The biologist E. O. Wilson once wrote, "Homo sapiens is the only species to suffer psychological exile." The removal of four hundred thousand acres of land from black hands, the inability to participate in government mandated processes such as the Homestead Act, being touted as the "missing link" and considered too "primitive" to be full citizens, and to die at the hands of those who believe they are morally justified in their actions, have left African Americans at times physically and psychologically exiled from their homeland while still in it (Trethewey 2010). When we consider the role that our public lands play in determining the national characteristics of this "homeland" and African Americans' engagement in this process, we can begin to understand what Outka meant when he said that it is difficult for African Americans to have an "uncomplicated union with the natural world" as compared to European Americans in the United States.

The "universalizing determination" to paint particular ideas of wilderness and the environment as the purview of all Americans obscures a messy racial past that denies the role of power and privilege in determining what meanings are prioritized and what experiences are made invisible (Penrose 2003). While no group of people is monolithic, it is integral to this exercise to call "whiteness" out in order to understand how race matters in the development of environmental ideas and policies in the United States. What is most important is to challenge the idea that "whiteness" is "a precondition of vision" and that a Euro-centric view is both normative and universal (Haraway 1989, 152).

In the Oscar-winning film *Dances with Wolves*, the director/actor Kevin Costner invites us to see American Indians through his eyes (complete with cultural commentary and political correctness) instead of Indians representing themselves from their perspective, one not grounded in a

Euro-American worldview (Hoffman 1997, 47). In this chapter, I invited the reader to imagine the collective African American experience through their eyes, in *relation* to a universalized Euro-American perspective, not through the lens of the collective white experience. In the 2010 article "The Reinvention of the Reverend" in *Newsweek* magazine on Al Sharpton and race in America, the authors, Allison Samuels and Jerry Adler, discussed what they understood as "the ways in which the respective histories of black and white give rise to unsettling divergent worldviews" (Samuels and Adler 2010, 24). I would like to offer a slightly different viewpoint. Our "histories" are not separate at all, but are really just one big complicated, messy story of our beginnings on this soil. We may collectively or individually have separate ways of seeing and experiencing our history, and we can choose to claim some parts of that history and not others. But through our institutions, our policies, our changing social mores and beliefs, we continue to navigate, negotiate, revisit, and revise the legacy of our multiple experiences in the United States.

From the beginning, the creation of "wilderness" and public lands (parks and forests) was the centerpiece to the nation-building project of defining who we are as Americans. These lands were our cathedrals, our representations to the world of, supposedly, the best of who we are and who we can be. From the beginning, African Americans as well as other nonwhite peoples were not allowed to participate on their own terms in this project. And when they were, the how, when, and where of their participation was determined by the dominant culture through legislation, rhetoric, science, and popular perception.

The legacy of American history as it relates to African Americans affects everyone. But for African Americans, the memory of slavery and segregation has manifested in many ways, including in the form of an emotional residue that has the capacity to be a roadblock in the pursuit of healthy human/environment relationships. So when you see a picture of a well-known black man in a pose similar to that of a large primate, there is a precedent for the reactions from members of the African American community. Charges of over-sensitivity fall flat when we begin to accept the legacy of the American story and what lies beneath our somewhat polished historic image. The picture of LeBron James is both a symbol of our inability to come to terms with our racialized past and a reminder that no matter how far or fast we move to our collective future, these moments in history remain embedded in the American unconscious, emerging in often painful, surprising, and sometimes unrecognizable ways.

in the contested meanings and representations of a green space designated as a national park. On a larger scale, it raises questions about how certain experiences and memories of the past are often rendered invisible in the present, both in institutions and on the landscape, and how African Americans experience the reverberations of this "forgetting" as well as the stories themselves.

How does memory, both collective and individual, shape African American environmental attitudes and perceptions? In this chapter, I will discuss two key periods of American history that highlight the complexity and contentiousness of African American environmental experience: slavery and the Jim Crow era. These two eras both resulted in explicit environmental practices by African Americans, from the avoidance of some places (e.g., the woods) to the creation of their own alternative outdoor places (e.g., Virginia Key Beach). Collective memory for African Americans has been shaped by these two historical moments (slavery and Jim Crow), and they continue to inform African American environmental participation today.

Critical race theory and black cultural studies offer crucial insights into understanding the African American environmental consciousness and the historic contingencies that have shaped that experience/process. While "race" is a contested category and has been variously described and debated by numerous scholars, critics, and public intellectuals, it has been used to contextualize the particular historical experience of blacks and whites, and their relationship to each other, in the United States in both the academic and popular imagination. Shackel (2003) explains that the concept of race "imposed social meaning on physical variations between human groups and served as a basis for structuring the total society" (3). In *The Miner's Canary*, Lani Guinier advocates the use of race as a diagnostic tool to check in on the state of the world. Emphasizing race and, in particular, racial identity highlights the relational aspects of people to each other and the places they live (Guinier and Torres 2002). Further, Michael Eric Dyson talks about "the collective racial unconsciousness, and the rhythms, relations, and rules of race" that inform all decision-making processes, even those that seem to have nothing to do with race (Dyson 2006, 20). He defines "rhythms" as the "customs and cultural practices that feed on differences between racial groups"; "relations" have to do "with the conditions that foster or frustrate interactions between racial groups"; and "rules" deal "with norms and behavior that reflect or resist formal barriers to social equality" (19). But while race implicitly or explicitly influences everyone, we are reminded that each racial category is comprised of subjects with diverse cultural identities and social experiences (Hall 1996). There is no single, authentic, essential African American experience.

In his recent work, *We Who Are Dark*, Tommie Shelby discusses the challenges of defining black identity and employs the different dimensions in the form of "thin and thick blackness." "Thin" blackness refers to certain visible physical characteristics that would signify a person as black. This includes the type of hair and the shape of the nose and lips. "Thick" blackness, on the other hand, which may include a component of thin blackness, is more complex. According to Shelby, "thick blackness can be adopted, altered, or lost through individual action" (2005, 209). It is comprised of five "modes" of blackness: racial, ethnic, national, cultural, and kindred. While all modes offer various options for understanding black identity, in this chapter I use the cultural concept "blackness," in which black identity is acknowledged as "an identifiable ensemble of beliefs, values, conventions, traditions, and practices" (211).

While these discussions make it impossible to answer with any certainty exactly how blackness is defined, few would argue about the national experience and social realities of being perceived as black that are experienced by most African Americans. As Shelby states, "the choice not to self-identify as black, whatever its rationale, does not dissolve the often constraining social realities that are created by the fact that others may insist on ascribing such an identity to one and consequently may treat one accordingly" (Shelby 2005, 213).

"Cultural trauma" refers to a "traumatic tear" that creates the need to "narrate new foundations," including reinterpreting and re-righting the past in order to reconcile present and future needs (Eyerman 2001). "Collective memory," the way a group of people "remember" the past, is used as a cognitive map to orient people's present behavior. Collective memory offers the opportunity to engage people's ideas, imaginings, and feelings about the past as a way of understanding how memory informs present actions and planning for the future (Irwin-Zarecka 1994). The historical narratives or "discourses of heritage" of African Americans are shaped by individual and collective remembrances that bind together families and communities (Toila-Kelly 2004). While diverse, the African American community is arguably "unified by enforced subordination and oppression" (Eyerman 2001, 14). Specifically, 250 years of slavery and a concerted effort by the United States government and legal system to legitimize Jim Crow laws have left scars that many are unwilling or unlikely to forget (Dyson 2006).

These traumatic experiences of the past are part of the cultural fabric of American identity in general and African American identity in particular. All efforts to reconcile "cultural trauma" in specific historical contexts involve identity and memory. The story of the Magnolia Plantation illustrates the value a site has, not just as a symbol of a tortured past, but as an indicator of the way memory is embedded in place. As Eyerman (2001) puts it, "The past becomes present through the embodied reactions of individuals as they carry on their daily lives" (5). Contemporary African Americans possess a geographical imagination that may be "bounded by inherited interpretive frames" (130). While the environmental narratives of a historically privileged few may have cultural and political sway over the majority, African Americans negotiate these narratives by inserting their own stories.

David Delaney uses the term "geographies of experience" to illustrate the link between the life experiences of individuals and the spatial organization of society where "significant commonalities among lives" exist (2002, 4). A fundamental aspect of a geography of experience is the way in which the individuals' choices, the context of these choices, and the resultant possibilities that do or do not materialize become part of individual and collective identities. For African Americans in the United States, complicit in creating a geography of experience, there are particular narratives born of shared memories and a collective identity that reflect a contested and often painful history. While arguably indispensable to understanding American national identity, these narratives do not always possess equal power to shape, inform, and create landscapes, institutions, and policies that, in turn, affect the attitudes, beliefs, and subsequent interactions of all individuals in general and black communities in particular. Dominant environmental narratives rarely reflect the different human and environment constructions that African Americans encounter, based on the historical context of their collective experience within the United States (Elder, Wolch, and Emel 1998). Instead, prominent views of the environment (whether forests, parks, or any other type of green space) while not unified, still draw from the experiences, values, and nationalistic desires of a privileged few who are in a position to influence and establish legitimacy for their ideas institutionally and culturally.

Though not a monolithic group, African Americans occupy a unique position within the creation/nexus of the American experience. While specificity of place, individual agency, and generational differences are not to be ignored, the very nature of the collective black experience in the United States (as one that is largely controlled by a white majority that defined everyday life according to their values and needs) highlights commonalities among African Americans, whose beliefs and attitudes were shaped in relation to this larger understanding. For many, the black experience is predominantly informed by a narrative of struggle (Dickerson 2004). Stories of African American life often reflect the experiences of black people struggling to be full human beings in spite of the legacy of slavery and Jim Crow. Whether in the form of resistance, self-improvement, or artistic expression, "the black collective response to white supremacy" is a reaction to the white gaze (Ogbar 2004, vii). For others, black life reflected something other than the "race problem." Zora Neale Hurston's anthropological work on black communities in Florida reflected her desire to describe a community that did not seem to define itself according to the dictates and desires of white America (Boyd 2003). Regardless of how black people collectively defined themselves in general, there was a link between the experiences had, the stories told, and a larger historical context within which their lives were embedded.[4]

COLLECTIVE MEMORY

According to Maurice Halbwachs, a well-known sociologist, collective memories are socially constructed by groups who remember or re-create specific events in the past (Coser 1992). "Memories, which constitute our own identity and provide context for every thought and action," are not just our own; they are borrowed, inherited, and learned and are part of a common experience kept alive by individuals, communities, cultures, and nations (Fentress and Wickham 1992, viii). Memory also constitutes a body of knowledge for the individual, and community memory becomes a way its members claim and own their past, particularly when their narratives are relegated to the margins of social and cultural importance. Memory becomes increasingly valuable to a group whose values are perceived to be morally threatening to the status quo, particularly when they are "presented as a legitimate perspective on social relations" (Sibley 1995, 132).

While scholars have explored collective memory in relation to political and international events such as the Holocaust, little research has focused on how collective memories may inform environmental interactions for African Americans (Johnson and Bowker 2004). While most African Americans have never seen a lynching, the act of terror perpetrated on a black person in the woods is remembered both for the place where it happened and the act itself. Evelyn C. White, an African American writer, believed her fear of hiking in the Oregon countryside was justified by the murder of Emmett Till in 1955 in Money, Mississippi (White 1996). For many Americans, the killing of a fourteen-year-old black boy for allegedly whistling at a white woman (his eyes were gouged out and he was thrown in a river with a seventy-nine-pound cotton gin strapped to his body) was a "primal event" that has had an "enduring presence in our collective memory" (Metress 2002, 3). For White, the picture of him in death was emblazoned on her memory: "I saw a reflection of myself and the blood-chilling violence that would greet me if I ever dared to venture into the wilderness" (White 1996, 285).[5]

It is not just the power of collective memories that shapes everyday interactions with the environment. African Americans invest a degree of trust in the "truth" inherent in those memories that they may not give to "facts" as expressed by "legitimate" institutions and popular media. "Distant statistics are certainly not as important as the actual experience of a sober person. We are, by reason of the lives we have led, suspicious people" (Gwaltney 1993, 7). Whether "remembering" the Tuskegee experiments or never receiving forty acres and a mule, many African Americans developed a deep mistrust of those institutions and individuals in positions of power.[6] But, according to White, for many African Americans, "there is a reclaiming process that can take place" that allows black people to keep a "sense of history" while fostering a sense of peace.[7]

Worster (1990) offers a framework to get at the meanings people attribute to the environment that are based on ideologies, beliefs, myths, and experiences. People make "cognitive maps" of the world around them, which are continually shifting, as are the values and ideologies that inform these maps. Collective and individual memory become part of this map, contributing to an individual's behavior and potentially affecting subsequent generations and ethnic identity formation (Johnson and Bowker 2004).

How do we understand the environmental practices and realities of a social/cultural group where specific historical processes have shaped that experience? Some argue that linear American narratives are used to obscure the complexity of green spaces, thereby denying the possibility of engagement (Wilson 2001). Euro-American attitudes about nature are largely expressed in a historical "model" that has "all the flexibility and variation of a conveyor belt; it gives very little room to variations in groups and individuals or in places or times" (Limerick 2000, 173). Whether intentional or not, many discussions on the relationship between "man" and the environment, while explicit about the details of that relationship, obscure exactly *which* "man" controlled and defined this relationship. There is often an unspoken, blanket assumption that the relationship is one without complexity—all humans operate under the same banner. For example, in *Landscape and Memory*, Schama talks about slavery as an expression of the great aristocracy's desire to make money. There is no mention of the involvement of the slave except as a backdrop to the white experience. Blacks are neither the "traditional cultures" who were living in "sacred reverence" with nature, nor the primary exploiters of the land (7).[8] What Schama offers is an environmental narrative that is sweeping, powerful, and explanatory on a macro scale, but limited in its ability to expose the messiness and multiple layers of experience between specific groups of humans, as well as between humans and the environment.

Narratives about the "natural environment" inform environmental interactions and shape the institutions concerned with environmental issues. But in a society where a dominant story shapes the way space is used and understood, the "limitations of the official story" reduce place-based differences and by implication, people's distinct experiences, to "the residual" and the marginal (Agnew and Smith 2002, 3).

In the early part of American history, when Africans were forcibly brought to the New World and sold as slaves, interaction with the natural environment was influenced by the economic incentives of the "master" class and by survival instinct. Between 1619 and the early 1800s, approximately four hundred thousand enslaved Africans were brought to the United States to work on plantations, in forests, and on water (as fishermen and boat builders). An additional 8 million were made to work the coffee and sugar plantations of Brazil and the Caribbean and the mines of Spanish America (Earle 2000, 23). They "girdled and fired trees, removed stumps and cultivated land, herded cattle . . . erected the hydraulic systems of banks, canals and drains . . . and planted, tended, harvested, and processed plantation crops throughout the colonies" (Stewart 2006, 10). In addition, they put to use relevant skills and knowledge previously developed in the irrigated rice fields of West Africa (Carney 2001). Working the land under the threat of the whip and the sun was an integral part of the "environmental experience" of enslaved Africans (Mellon 1988). Through backbreaking labor and general day-to-day interactions, enslaved Africans became more knowledgeable about their surrounding environment than their white slave owners (Stewart 2006).

While slaves spent the majority of their time laboring on the land, not all their environmental interactions were related to work.[9] The knowledge about their environment obtained through work afforded slaves an intimate understanding of the places where they lived that they used in their hunting, in cultivating their personal gardens, and in the raising of their livestock (Stewart 2006). Combining ingenuity and necessity while drawing on their cultural heritage, slaves devised numerous methods for successfully catching animals and fish to supplement their meager diets. Hunting and fishing provided food, money, material goods, and community-building activities for enslaved Africans (Giltner 2006). "Wild resources," those animals and plants culled from woods and waterways, were also used by individuals to increase their power within the slave community and between master and slave (Stewart 2006, 14). In particular, the wild environment was a source of power for female slaves who were knowledgeable about roots and herbs used for medicinal purposes (Blum 2002). Cultivating and foraging plants was also a form of resistance—a way for slaves to regain and maintain ownership over their bodies and how they cared for them (Stewart 2006; Blum 2002).

Africans believed in "good use" of the land and the connection between the health of the land and their community (Blum 2002). The "woods" induced both positive and negative feelings: a place that was resource-rich, a place of transformation and refuge (forests were often used for religious services), but also a place to fear (Blum 2002; Dixon 1987). Forced labor was often regulated through the threat or actual use of physical violence, and the fear engendered through mental and emotional trauma was another constant that enslaved Africans had to contend with in relation to the natural environment. White women put fear into the hearts of slaves about the woods in order to maintain control.[10] Whites also told slaves stories suggesting they were "like animals" in the woods, in order to keep them thinking of themselves as subhuman (Blum 2002).

Africans and Native Americans recognized that plants, animals, and humans all had a place in the world and should be treated with a respect that acknowledged the interdependence of all things. This view contrasted with widespread beliefs among white men at that time who felt that nature should be dominated and exploited for profit and who espoused a form of Christianity that supported the separation of humans from nature (Merchant 1989). Enslaved African women also saw these "natural spaces" as places where gender and racial power played out along with fear and control. Though understanding that their interactions with nature allowed them some power in black and white society, enslaved African women were not able, like their white female counterparts, to significantly engage in the public realm (Blum 2002).

Animals and natural occurrences such as shooting stars also terrified many enslaved Africans (Blum 2002). But for the most part, these fears did not overshadow the horror of being whipped and kept in chains. Many runaway slaves used the woods to hide, sometimes only for a brief respite from slave life or as a permanent refuge (Blum 2002; Simpson 1990). Still for others, the forest marked the beginning of their journey to freedom. For example, the Great Dismal Swamp, a wetland expanse covering six hundred square miles in Virginia and North Carolina, became home for hundreds of runaway slaves (or maroons) in the early nineteenth century (Simpson 1990). Despite the difficulty of navigating this kind of terrain, runaway slaves shared their knowledge of this environment with each other to build a life apart from the watchful gaze of their white owners while successfully avoiding capture (Simpson 1990). Over seventy-five thousand slaves are said to have run away from their life of bondage (Earle 2000, 60). Today their experiences are commemorated by the National Park sites that contain pieces of the Underground Railroad.[11]

For blacks and whites in the antebellum South, particularly in the rural areas, "identity was rooted in the land" (Eyerman 2001, 35). For African Americans, the lack of participation with and overall feeling of disconnectedness from the environment may have found its "birth" in the slave experience (Johnson and Bowker 2004, 65). For many of the African American interviewees who participated in my research, slavery played a role in how they perceived different aspects of their natural environment. While only 40 percent of those I interviewed listed "stigma associated with slavery" high on their list as a potential factor influencing African American environmental participation, nearly all interviewees spoke about the power of the past and their belief that slavery had some influence on people's attitude toward the natural environment.[12] "We've had so many atrocious things happen to us in the woods" laments Leola McCoy, a Floridian who resided in Fort Lauderdale.[13] To combat this fear and the subsequent "psychological divorce" from the environment that many African Americans feel, black park rangers emphasize the importance of interpreting black history as an explicit part of the National Parks narrative.[14] African American Betty Reid Soskin, who at age ninety is believed to be the oldest National Park ranger, adds that "what gets remembered is a function of whose in the room doing the remembering."[15]

After the abolition of slavery in the late nineteenth century, African Americans experienced a surge in opportunities and possibilities of all kinds. But the post-slavery black experience could be labeled a circumscribed freedom at best. At the end of the Civil War in 1865, on his march through the South, William Tecumseh Sherman granted an army mule and forty acres of land along the southeastern coast to freed blacks. The "forty acres and a mule" program represented only a temporary vision, however, as President Andrew Johnson soon revoked the order and the lands were returned to their white former owners. With the passage of Jim Crow segregation laws beginning in 1875 in Tennessee, the "separate but equal" mandates that many states upheld determined where African Americans could congregate.[16] Lethal violence toward black people came primarily in the form of lynching (Earle 2000). In nearly every state in the union and particularly in the South, black people were subject to extralegal actions that often resulted in their death by hanging. A tree became a painful symbol for many black people, reminding them that the color of their skin could mean death.[17] "The tree is associated with lynching," states MaVynee Betsch matter-of-factly, a descendent of the African American founder of American Beach near Jacksonville, Florida.[18] This should be no surprise; between 1882 and 1968, approximately 4,742 black people were lynched illegally by white mobs (Litwack 2004, 12). Approximately the same number of people were either legally lynched (based on court decisions), fell victims to "private white violence," or were murdered by a variety of means in isolated rural sections and dumped in river and creeks (Litwack 2004, 12). Lynching was primarily designed to curtail the freedom of movement and occupation that African Americans had begun to enjoy, and some commentators suggest that "lynchings will remain in the public discourse as a vague symbol of black oppression" (Brundage 2000, 338). Arguably, lynching succeeded in limiting the environmental imagination of black people whose legitimate fear of the woods served as a painful and very specific reminder that there are many places a black person should not go. For African Americans, traveling to and from outdoor areas, particularly parks and forests, it is easier today than it was during the Jim Crow era, when extra precautions were taken to avoid traveling through "hostile white terrain" (P. West 1993, 112). But examples still persist that illustrate how spatial mobility for African Americans can be limited by a lingering concern for their safety while crossing through territory deemed "white." Planners working for Gateway Park in New York City (part of the NPS system), expressed frustration over their inability to convince inner-city minority youths to visit the park, as the teenagers do not want to travel through "miles and miles of upper middle class terrain to get to the park" (113). In the *New York Times*, a self-described middle-class African American woman spoke about the concerns her family had about taking a proposed driving vacation through Montana (Belk 2003). Her fifteen-year old son put it this way: "Four black folks from Oakland, California cruising the back roads of Montana. Are you nuts?" (Belk 2003, 25). Echoing this sentiment, one interviewee reminded me that "If we're not afraid, we're crazy."[19]

Segregation was expressed and experienced in a number of ways. Black people were limited by several factors: where they could find employment, attend school, socialize, and live (Earle 2000). The environmental sector, specifically natural resource management, was also affected by segregation. When the Civilian Conservation Corps (CCC) was founded as one of President Franklin D. Roosevelt's New Deal agencies, it was deemed a successful effort at providing men and youth with jobs while practicing conservation. But CCC work camps were segregated, and many of the all-black CCC camps were unwelcome by communities across the country, including California (Cole 1999). In addition, other federal and state agencies including the Forest Service and the NPS were often complicit because of their partnerships with the CCC (Cole 1999).

While the erosion of Jim Crow laws (beginning with the 1954 Supreme Court decision outlawing segregation in public schools) hit its stride in the 1960s, some aspects of segregation continue in the present (Earle 2000). In *Sundown Towns: A Hidden Dimension of American Racism*, James Loewen explores the existence of organized jurisdictions that prevented African Americans from living within their boundaries. According to Loewen, the old saying goes that a "nigger" better not find himself or herself in one of these towns after sundown. Sundown towns could be found across the country; many African Americans accepted that towns with "white" in their name were signaling their sundown status (Loewen 2005).[20] Wealthy white suburbs continued the trend of actively excluding black families in implicit and explicit ways, sometimes by using existing natural landmarks. Rock Creek Park in Washington, D.C., the largest urban park in the National Park system separates Chevy Chase, a wealthy white enclave "from the increasingly black neighborhoods" proliferating on the nearby landscape of Maryland (Loewen 2005, 124). In addition, while there has been an increase in middle- and upper-middle-class black families that live near the park, according to one NPS employee that I interviewed, there is some disagreement between white and black community members over how the park should be used. Black people wanted the option to use the park as a commuter route while white people did not. It is also seen as a high crime area, and there are "racial stigmas" attached to the park that are sometimes expressed by other NPS employees.[21]

Segregation in the early twentieth century was legally supported and explicitly expressed on the landscape, shaping mobility patterns and social behavior. While these laws have been abolished and any explicit social behavior supporting separation based on race is openly condemned by the law and popular opinion, one does not need to see a "whites only" sign to feel that he or she is not welcome. Intentionally or not, manipulation of the natural landscape combined with an infusion of values and beliefs of a group of individuals with the power to define their reality on their own terms works just as well.

CLAIMING OUR OWN: *Narratives of Struggle in Florida*

For African Americans doing historical research, interpreting and understanding individual experience or "biography" through the lens of historical consciousness dates back to the nineteenth century. The Reverend J. W. C. Pennington, a Presbyterian minister and fugitive slave, published *A Text Book on the Origins and History . . . of the Colored People* (Bethel 1999). Along with other historical treatises, it helped shape a tradition of historical inquiry that linked individual memory to a collectively remembered past in order to define an African American identity. Through this process, "the individual and the autobiographical is collectivized and generalized" (168). W. E. B. Du Bois's seminal work, *The Souls of Black Folk*, has been called a "memory palace" underscoring the power the text has for students, writers, and others who turn and return to "*Souls*" for assistance in remembering their collective past (Blight 1994, 54).

For many black communities across the United States, remembering by legitimizing historic sites through national, state, and local agencies becomes a way of reconciling their past with the present. For a population that has seen its collective past submerged or erased from the American narrative, seeing a piece of history on the landscape is an opportunity for them to better understand who they are and where they've come from. Additionally, a historic site that symbolizes the pain and injustice of slavery and segregation offers a chance for healing and reconciliation.

Stories of environmental experiences for many African Americans are often explicitly embedded in the larger historical context in which they took place. While beaches represent pleasure and evoke images of tranquility, the reality of a Jim Crow South dictated that race was a defining factor in who was allowed to experience all that a beach had to offer (Mormino 2005). One example was the creation of Virginia Key Beach in Miami,

Florida. During World War II, the U.S. Navy recruited African Americans. But there was no beach in Miami where black sailors could train. Consequently, in 1944, the Dade County Commission gave permission for creation of a temporary beach exclusively for black sailors (Dunn 1997). But in 1945, blacks pushed to have a permanent beach for all black community members. They organized a "wade-in" at the "white's only" Baker's Haulover Beach, marking the beginning of the civil rights movement in Dade County. On August 1, 1945, the "black beach" which encompassed eighty-two acres of shoreline, nature trails, and indigenous and exotic tree species, was opened. Thousands of black people visited the beach each year (Dunn 1997). Virginia Key Beach eventually became integrated, and in 1982, the park closed for two decades. In 1999, a "trust" was established to restore the park and beach. In 2002, the site was listed on the National Register of Historic Places because of its significance to black and Floridian history. Through locally held meetings, decisions were made concerning the nature of the restoration process, which will include a collection of oral histories from individuals who frequented the beach in the 1940s and 1950s. Guy Forchion, the assistant executive director of the Virginia Key Beach Trust, emphasized the need to acknowledge that Virginia Key Beach "was a safe space" where black people could get away from racism.[22] For many of the surviving African Americans, "re-identifying with Virginia Key helped revive their memories of place within a political culture where black historical consciousness and power had been limited" (Bush 2006, 165).

Another example of a community remembering itself in place is the ongoing effort by black and white Floridians to preserve and protect American Beach on Amelia Island, near Jacksonville. Spearheaded by MaVynee Betsch, the beach was designated as *the* premier black beach resort in the 1940s by her great-grandfather, Abraham Lincoln Lewis. It was frequented by the rich as well as the working class and was known as a place where black society could find respite from the stress of living in the Jim Crow South (Rymer 1998). According to Betsch, American Beach did not become threatened until the 1980s when developers started buying lots. "Developers are entrenched here now," she lamented.[23] But so was Betsch. Returning to American Beach after living for years in Europe, she inherited her great-grandfather's house and eventually was inspired to give away all of her wealth to environmental causes (Rymer 1998). While her environmental interests initially took on an international direction, she eventually turned her sights to her home; she had grown concerned that both the natural environment and the cultural history of the place would be lost.

Single-handedly, Betsch brought attention to the importance of recognizing the beach as a font of African American history and enlisted numerous community members, local, state, and national organizations to her cause. Sadly, Betsch passed away in September of 2005. But not before she succeeded in convincing the National Park Service to bring eight acres of sand dunes that run along the beach under the park's protection.

Some challenge that African Americans are not able to "remember" how the woods were also a place of spiritual rejuvenation or other positive experiences because these moments in our collective history are overshadowed by more recent memories that emphasized choices made in relation to the white experience. According to native Floridian Bernadette Clayborne, African Americans still wear the "emotional chains" of the past. "We've been stigmatized," she admits. In addition, these positive stories are buried, marginalized, or forgotten by those in a position to shape the environmental movement. For African Americans involved in the restoration of Virginia Key Beach and American Beach, it is not so much the preservation or conservation of the natural environment that motivates their activism or participation. Collective and individual memory is "redefining public purpose in our times" (Bush 2006). Remembering and re-creating Virginia Key Beach and American Beach is a way to acknowledge the African American experience and a way for African Americans to acknowledge themselves. It is part of a healing process that satisfies the desire to build "a secure place . . . for one's ancestral memory" (Da Vasquez 2001, 161). "People and things come to stand for each other." African Americans see Virginia Key Beach as an environment that reflects the past, the present, and themselves (Sibley 1995, 10).

In the United States, there is sometimes a desire to hold on to the "good old days" of the past. We linger in memories that provide us some comfort because of their familiarity, particularly in times when the present is contentious and the future uncertain. While neo-conservatives have been charged with this behavior by others on the opposite end of the political spectrum, African Americans are also in danger of finding security in the anger and loss of the past.[24] This "holding on" robs them of the possibility of addressing their own agency and developing the skills to create change. This assertion is not to deny the power of structural processes and systemic issues that shape our day-to-day decisions and possibilities. But, if the components that make up identity (who we are) are not static, then it follows that our ability to take action (the power that we have), changes according to the given situation/context. Historically, the African American has developed the skills to assimilate and know the "master's" needs and character in order to survive. However, I suggest that African Americans on the whole have not also developed to the same extent the skill to nurture their own needs grounded in their own imaginations outside of the white gaze.

According to many African Americans that I spoke to while attending environmental workshops and in interviews, holding on to these feelings can express itself in terms of environmental action and participation in three ways:

1. Anger, while justified, can result in resistance to new ideas or a re-fusal to consider anything that doesn't appear to directly address the anger. The anger becomes part of people's identity, and they fear if they lose that, they have nothing, no power. Anger becomes the only vehicle in which to explore their feelings and thoughts around these issues, but it is often damaging to others and to themselves.

2. Fatigue, tired of being asked to explain the "black experience" in rela-tion to environmental issues, leads some African Americans to resist participating in events largely seen as white and where they feel they are expected to "represent" the race. They tire of having that conver-sation with white people. Without the conversation, the dialogue is at a standstill.

3. Mistrust of outsiders often causes rejection of those African Ameri-cans who are seen as "gatekeepers." This includes people who work for organizations or institutions not considered "grassroots" who come into a community where they are not members. They may be seen as representatives of those in power as opposed to potential work mates/collaborators.

In her book *Shifting the Ground*, Rachel Stein describes "turning some-thing over" as a "process of investigation . . . in order to gain a fuller view of what has been hidden from sight" (1997, 3). In turn, revelation results in the ground shifting to accommodate a "new planting" and a new relationship between a person, the environment, and history. African Americans and those in a position to influence environmental institutions have an op-portunity to expand existing environmental narratives to consider a more complex history that reflects the confluence of diverse experiences, beliefs, and ideas.

In this chapter, I have highlighted how the dominant environmental narrative in the United States, grounded in the notion that uninhabited wilderness areas represent American identity and need to be preserved, does not adequately address collective African American experiences in relation to natural landscapes. The exclusion or marginalization of African American stories in the management of green spaces denies environmental institutions and organizations the ability to understand how diverse environmental practices are influenced by individual and collective memories experienced by African Americans. I suggest that for African Americans, creating a deep-seated sense of feeling and responsibility regarding the environment may not come primarily from telling them they need to save the trees for their children's future (this isn't meant to imply that they don't care about their children's future). Recent history shows that African Americans are continually using the past as a way to represent themselves and say, "we were there" and "we are here now." Why should it be any different when talking about the environment? Specifically, for African Americans, memory, both collective and individual, provides a way to name and re-create a place, which gives or reaffirms the power to re-create ourselves and the places we live in. This allows us to construct *environmental spaces* in our own image.

Today on the Magnolia Plantation, as part of their visit to Louisiana's Cane River Creole National Historical Park, guests learn how African American slaves tilled the land, built the shops, and created the landscape that is preserved. After the Civil War, freed slaves and their descendants remained as tenant farmers and sharecroppers; they continued to shape the land and its Creole culture. African American park rangers evoke memories of slave and sharecropper experiences as integral to the deep history of the plantation itself.

Focusing on preserving a piece of the past is a way to say, "We were there" and indirectly allows for more control and power in deciding (collectively?) who we were and who we *are*. Consequently, memory, as a way of evoking the past, becomes an important vehicle for involving the community in environmental preservation, conservation, and participation.

In addition, there needs to be recognition by environmental institutions that memory and personal experience for many African Americans far outweigh the "distant statistics" that do not reflect their lives. While I am not suggesting discarding statistics in favor of anecdotes when making policy decisions, I do advocate for inclusion of personal stories in any decision-making process that is truly interested in diversity. Not only would this addition be indicative of an institution's willingness to expand and include, it could be a tool toward building coalitions within and across communities for addressing local and national environmental concerns.

CHAPTER FOUR

Black Faces

I think it is critical that people document . . . really begin to
consciously think about all the holes that we have, again because
so much of the history is an oral tradition and because we need proof.

—Ayoka Chenzira, interviewed in Klotman and Cutler (1999)

I know we've come a long way baby, but it seems like we've hardly moved.

—Environmentalist Audrey Peterman (interview with author, January 2003)

Hurricane Katrina is considered one of the worst natural disasters in our country's history. On August 29, 2005, the first Category 5 hurricane of the year slammed into Louisiana and Mississippi, leading to a breach in the 17th Street canal levee in New Orleans and flooding the entire Ninth Ward (Dyson 2006). Images of displaced water and people evoked a sense of helplessness, anger, despair, and shock across the nation and many parts of the world. While we were stunned by Nature's destructiveness, something else, perhaps more insidious, was taking place.[1] The images of black people "looting" and "shooting" during this desperate time were recorded and shown worldwide, providing an explicit image with an implicit meaning: "logics constructed in visual images that define blackness" (Rogers 1994, 160). These "logics," the idea that there is an essential and fixed quality to blackness (in the case of Katrina, criminality and poverty), are represented as natural and normative behavior by simply and repeatedly showing these images. The power that images and words have in stigmatizing a people or community can have far-reaching psychological and material consequences. How one's identity is constructed through representations calls into question whose social realities are maintained and sustained by such representations and who benefits from the perpetuation of these depictions.[2]

Equally disturbing is how one perspective of an experience, a person, or a place, in this case African Americans of the Ninth Ward, can become so embedded in our consciousness through representational acts that we cannot imagine, and therefore do not act on, other possibilities for those phenomena we seek to understand. In addition, for the individuals who are being "represented," there is a danger of internalizing negative images to the extent that they cannot imagine different possibilities for themselves. Who we are and what we do is partially determined by our worldview; that perspective is informed by the stories we are told and the images we see. Many Americans "continued to be socialized via mass media and non-progressive educational systems" that privilege a worldview that demeans and devalues alternate ways of experiencing the world (hooks 1992, 18). In the case of Katrina, the images not only "tested the nation's collective sense of reality" but reminded us of our collective racial unconscious from which we take cues to determine our actions, including leaving "poor black folk defenseless before the fury of nature" (Dyson 2006, 19).

These representations underscore how "hegemonic power actively produces and reproduces difference" in order to "maintain social and spatial divisions that are advantageous to its continued empowerment"(Soja and Hooper 1993, 184). In this case, it is the power of the dominant narratives that are fundamental to our environmental institutions and policies. Compared to Katrina, the absence of more inclusive interpretive exhibits or diversity policies within environmental organizations seem almost benign. But over the long term, the narrow representation of African Americans or their outright invisibility within an environmental context produces similar consequences to those of Katrina: lack of awareness among a community's constituents, exclusivity and marginalization often interpreted as racism, and historical narratives lacking in complexity or unequal power relations resulting in unequal access to resources and exposure to highly vulnerable and/or hazardous environments with unequal resources to mitigate those hazards.

Representation and racialization sustain the way many Americans think about the natural environment in the United States, which informs our environmental policies, institutions, and interactions. Both processes have the power to determine who participates in environment-related activities and who does not; what voices are heard in environmental debates and what voices are not. The process of representation "always involves power relations and is mediated through historically changing institutions, class structures, taken-for-granted historical accounts and scientific assumptions" to shape today's reality through the remembered or revised reality of the past (Duncan 1993, 53). The power of representation lies in its ability to shape today's reality through that reality of the past (Moscovici 2001).

Using this conceptual framework to understand how "environment" is constructed in the United States brings into question the nature of the visual representation of African Americans in popular magazines that focus on environmental issues and/or the Great Outdoors, National Park exhibits and materials, and textual representation in these spaces—stories/narratives that shape and support our understanding of these green spaces (and each other). Pictures are used to "reinforce the credibility of stories." Stories become the vehicles we use to define ourselves and the places we inhabit and utilize. So, whose stories are being told? Whose pictures do we see? What messages are being given? Who is being targeted? Through what processes are these meanings/representations channeled to the public? The "possibility to make visible" is a concrete form of power. What about the person who is made visible or invisible? Invisibility is not a mere default, but can be part of an active process.

This chapter explores how the paucity of visual and textual representations of African Americans in popular media, the National Parks, and environmental education perpetuates their invisibility in conversations about environmental management. What follows is a brief look at the history of black representation in the popular media including television, magazines, and film. I examine the National Park Service with an eye toward exploring how African Americans have been represented in park brochures and interpretive exhibits. In addition, I present evidence that African Americans' concerns and interests in relation to the environment have not been articulated, invited, or understood in the accepted context of the environmental movement and natural resource management. Finally, I address how, within the context of the "environment," black identity is narrowly defined or poorly articulated and often results in limited interest and participation by African Americans in projects or work having to do with the environment.

> Going to the Lake District over the years . . . deliberately searching out England's timeworn countryside . . . searching the postcard-stand for the card that shows a sunny upland scene with a black person standing, looking over the hill. Never finding it. I fantasize about encountering that image. . . . Simple stories, simple connections. (Pollard 2004, 58)

So goes Ingrid Pollard's photographic exploration of black experience beyond the urban environment. As a black photographer, she weaves together historical narratives, memory, experience, and the theoretical in search of new expression of black experience in nature. While most of her work is centered on England, common themes suggest the importance of exploring the links among representation, African American experience, and place in the United States. She alludes to the power of seeing a black face pictured among England's "craggy rocks, rushing streams and lowly sheep" and how that image would have the power to connect her to place and expand her notion of self and black identity (2004, 58).

Pollard is not the first to explore the role of representation in defining or expanding notions of black identity. Stuart Hall (1997) posits that individuals give meaning to people and places "by our use of things; and what we say, think and feel about them—*how we represent them*" (my emphasis). Furthermore, "meaning is what gives us a sense of our own identity, of who we are and with whom we 'belong'" (3). As a signifying practice, representation is both political and formative. It has the power to shape attitudes, beliefs, and practices in part by the emotions that it evokes that feed on our fears, anxieties, and desires. As Hall explains, we are challenged to consider the multiple meanings behind any given image in order to understand that a representational practice often works to "fix" one meaning of an image while it privileges another. This allows us to question which meaning those with representational authority are privileging and for what purpose.

In addition, with respect to race, Hall (1997) argues that people who are "significantly different from the majority" are subject to a binary form of representation—good/bad, civilized/primitive—and that their degree of "cultural belongingness and difference" is potentially inscribed in any representation (230). Furthermore, one representation or image does not reflect only one moment in time. While some specificity of meaning can be attached to a singular image, striations of accumulated meaning run through that image that reflect the cultural differences at any particular historical moment. One image is often referential to another as a consequence of the repetition of representational practices in what is called "intertextuality." Relying on other images to support and legitimize an image's meaning creates a "regime of representation" that is difficult to resist, dismantle, or transform (232).

Historically, African Americans have struggled over self-definition and with their representations in the media (including movies, television, radio, books, newspapers, magazines, paintings, sculptures, etc.). According to Hall (1997), there were three historic moments when the "'West' encountered black people," prompting representations "marking racial difference": when Europeans made contact with West Africa in the sixteenth century for the primary purpose of acquiring slaves, during the spread of European colonization in Africa, and as people from the developing world migrated to the West after World War II (239). Representations of "primitive" Africans were used to perpetuate and sustain the ideas and values of the West that supported economic growth while at the same time reflecting the feelings and thoughts that justified actions of moral superiority and shaped the social imagination. Whether they were images of the white explorer's encounters with the African exotic, the happy "darkie" with his white master, or the stereotype of a black person with caricatured big lips and broad nose, popular representations of black people were effective at essentalizing black identity and emphasizing black difference.[3] For black people, it has meant struggling against externalized and internalized oppression.

"The field of representation (how we see ourselves, how others see us) is a site of ongoing struggle" (hooks 1994, 46). This struggle is expressed in a number of ways: in the desire to be seen, the struggle for expression, the need for resources to support a different representational vision of blackness, and as a forum to express social and political tensions (Klotman and Cutler 1999). For a significant part of American history (well into the twentieth century), black representation was controlled largely by white men whose own agendas required the naturalizing of difference. By "fixing" difference and determining that difference to be "natural" as opposed to cultural, these representational authorities have ensured that black representations are then "beyond history, permanent and fixed" and are relegated to an ideological and discursive place where meaning is protected from the possibility of change (Hall 1997, 245).

INCOGNEGRO

Numerous examples of this fixed imagery abound. Uncle Tom was the very essence of the "good," faithful black slave. Aunt Jemima was the quintessential black mammy; with her kerchief on her head and her bountiful breasts secured by her apron, she graced the outside of pancake boxes and syrup bottles, as well as our imagination (Manring 1998). There were gollywogs and minstrels, Uncle Remus and "tricksters," all stereotypes that signified racial difference by attempting to reduce blackness to essential characteristics such as laziness, childishness, and faithfulness (Hall 1997). While contemporary imagery has experienced some changes that reflect larger sociohistorical moments, the representation of the black experience in the media is still imbued with stereotypes that wallow in the essentialism of the past. Whether it's the whore (which can range from a "loose woman" to a prostitute), gangsta, drug dealer, or rap singer, for many critics black representation still suffers from embedded beliefs of black essentialism and the need to signify difference.[4]

Stereotypes constrain representations of African Americans by reducing black people to a few essential characteristics, thereby limiting their ability as individuals to fully realize who they are (Finney 2003). By refusing to acknowledge the complexity of a black individual's lived experience, one is implicitly denying the possibilities of expanding consciousness that is arguably the birthright of all humans. As a consequence, the articulation of one's lived experience in the material world becomes stunted and constrained by that interpretation/vision.

Misrepresentation can be equally detrimental to personal development. One need look no further than Donald Bogle's *Toms, Coons, Mulattoes, Mammies and Bucks: An Interpretive History of Blacks in American Films* to begin to understand how these negative and stereotypical representations of black folk and black life could stir up feelings of inadequacy, anger, and embarrassment.[5] As black individuals consider their "place" in the American experience, these images have the power to set limitations within the mind and the world at large by constructing belief systems and understandings that use these images as touchstones (Figure 3). While bell hooks (1994) speaks of trying to "see myself beyond all the received images" in order to develop a healthy sense of self-worth, she also emphasizes the need to consider who is constructing these images and how these images have been affected by their own racism or internalized oppression (44).

Misrepresentation can also have consequences for the health and growth of a community. Marquetta Goodwine is the elected chieftess of the Gullah/Geechee nation, an enclave of African Americans of West African descent who live primarily along the southeastern coast of the United States. The coastline from South Carolina to northern Florida is home to an estimated three hundred thousand Gullah. The Gullah live in coastal South Carolina and the Geechee (named after the Ogeechee River in Georgia) live along the Georgia and Florida coast. Known fondly as Queen Quet, Goodwine spoke of her concern for the misinformation and misrepresentations about the Gullah that have been perpetrated on them by some researchers, film directors, and museums.[6] At best, this misrepresentation

Figure 3. White House and watermelons.

can present itself as a director's desire to present the culture according to his/her aesthetic as opposed to how the people actually view themselves. These misrepresentations can be received by the Gullah community as a slight or sign of disrespect. At worst, misrepresentation arising from mis-interpretations of their traditions can instill "condemnation and pity of Gullah-speaking Sea Islanders." "Those who do not understand the unique community that has been formed in the Sea Islands by the Gullahs and Geechees often regard its members as ignorant, barbaric, and backwards in their speech and practices" (Goodwine 1998, 9). When a community begins to feel that their language and practices are not "acceptable" in mainstream American society, that community may begin to devalue its own beliefs and traditions, forsaking the values and practices that are central to its identity. Many Gullah migrate to northern cities, leaving behind a way of speaking, a focus on "communalness," and land that has been in their community for many years. Ultimately, many Gullah feel that they have turned their back on their history and culture.

For the Gullah people, their way of life and collective sense of self is largely determined by their land, their relationship to it, and their ability to participate in resource management decision-making processes. However, their self-imposed separation from their past in order to "get ahead" in the present challenges their ability to fight the developers who are eager to buy their land for resorts and summer homes.[7] Misrepresentations have created barriers to potential alliances with outsiders to ward against developers who want to purchase Gullah land. By viewing Gullah language and traditions as inadequate to the task of living contemporary American lives, the Gullah run the risk of relinquishing their ability to rebuild the African American community they call home.

Resistance has come in many forms. For some black actors trapped in stereotypical film roles, it has meant finding a way to be subversive within those borders and present a more complex black representation. As one of the most well-known black actresses of the 1930s, and the first to win an Oscar, Hattie McDaniel epitomized the mammy and mother figure in her numerous roles as a servant. While many criticized McDaniel for accepting these roles, she used the opportunities to express her disdain for her white masters while being anything but submissive (Bogle 1992).[8] For more contemporary artists, scholars, and writers, the struggle has centered on the creation of works that are more explicit in imagining black life on its own terms (Klotman and Cutler 1999). Whether it is documentation based on "reality" (documentary film, essays, academic research) or the re-creation of existing narratives (for example, Alice Randall's parody of *Gone with the Wind*), African Americans have articulated their resistance in various forms with variable impact. These actions challenge the idea that identity is a static category and instead champion the idea of multiple identities while harshly interrogating those voices that have historically constructed an image of African Americans rooted in their own limitations and desires.

THIS LAND WAS MADE FOR YOU AND ME . . .

Representations of African Americans not only shape their imagination, but also inform the imagination of Americans as a whole. As images flash across a television screen or stare up at us from a magazine, they appear to be clues about the person represented, how that person behaves in the world, and how he or she relates to others. Our collective imagination is challenged by an American narrative of freedom, individualism, and honor that does not stand up well to competing narratives that consider for example, slavery and the removal of Native Americans from their lands. Justification for these actions is partially supported by negative imagery of

African Americans (and Native Americans) that portrays them as limited in what they can do and who they can become. As such, negative representations have fueled systemic institutional processes of racialization that implicitly or explicitly exclude African Americans from full participation that is touted to be the birthright of all Americans.

In her article on African Americans and their changing status in the American collective identity, Rebecca Kook (1998) looks at the symbolic manifestations of African American inclusion in that American collective identity. Arguing that the assumption that an American collective identity is not grounded in ethnicity, historical particularities, or cultural traditions, but more on citizenship, she points out how African Americans were routinely excluded from participating in the spoils that American collective identity afforded others. What resulted was a portrayal of American collective identity that is largely "static and nonchanging" and a sense that who African Americans are collectively is something different or outside of what is considered the norm (158). Kook goes on to say:

> To a very large degree, the construction of a collective identity is essentially an act of constructing and reconstructing the nation's past. Moreover, the essence of inclusion is . . . the act of official recognition. Recognition of identity—group or individual—is essential to the formation of one's identity. Similarly, the lack of such recognition, or the misrecognition of identity, bars the path to the development of a collective identity. (158)

In the United States, according to scholar Melissa Harris-Perry (2011), African Americans in the past and the present have confronted and engaged "representation that distorts their humanity" (think back to the image of LeBron James on the cover of *Vogue*). This "distortion" becomes a kind of misrecognition that "hinders the ability of black people to act as citizens" (19). The capacity of institutions with policies designed to motivate and escalate diverse public engagement in civic society is hindered by perceptions and beliefs that have been informed by these distortions. "What you see is what you get" becomes a kind of modus operandi that not only denies the humanity of those who are maligned, but limits the ability of these institutions to fully serve an increasingly diverse public. In the past, these images "sought to reaffirm the notion of blacks on the bottom at a time when war, Reconstruction, and immigration were shuffling the deck and putting the nature of national identity in question"

(Williams-Forson 2006, 51). In the present, these distortions can impede the ability of some people to accept that a black man is the president or imagine that an African American seen "looting" a store during the time of an environmental disaster is simply taking what is absolutely necessary for survival.[9]

A significant part of this American collective identity, particularly in relation to place, is grounded in the dominant narratives of environment and the Great Outdoors. Photographs of American wilderness that fuse "national identity and human spirit" have been offered "as a way to preserve the American landscape and save the American soul" (Dunaway 2005, xv). Dutch sailors, when first laying eyes on the east coast of what would become New York, are said to have seen the landscape as "an opportunity, a promise, a future" (Vale 1995, 11). But while all individuals may imbue a landscape with meaning, only some meanings gain traction in our quest to define ourselves and the places we live, or to shape a national narrative that supposedly reflects the beliefs and experiences of all Americans. We are less anxious to acknowledge that in order to have achieved certain goals on the road to become a nation, American identity was also informed by how some people "Othered" particular groups to advance certain tenets of Americanism, including economic freedom and prosperity. Whether we leave out the removal of American Indians from their land, or the refusal to give ex-slaves their forty acres and a mule, the effort to airbrush the definition of an American collective identity on the national landscape has stymied our ability to fully comprehend who Americans are collectively and individually.

There is a tension between an "American ideal of a color-blind national identity" and the identity of sub-groups, such as African Americans whose history and experience does not fully jibe with current values and beliefs (Agnew and Smith 2002, 231). The danger lies in how this tension becomes obscured in the pursuit of the larger objective. According to hooks (1992), claiming color-blindness allows an individual to have no responsibility or "accountability for anti-racist change" and frees the individual from having to consider different ways of experiencing the world (14). Consequently, the lack of recognition of "different" identities that have not historically fit into the broadly drawn American identity ideal has meant limited visions of who Americans are as a nation. Saying "Americans are all the same" becomes another way of perpetuating a narrative that privileges the white experience. In addition, representations of the wilderness as indicative of American identity have not embraced the complexity of the African American identity and in some cases have rendered it invisible.

IN OUR OWN IMAGE: *Environmental Imagery in the United States*

In exploring the impact of images on American environmental reform, Dunaway talks about the camera as a "technology of memory" and representation. While some photographers saw the camera as "objective" in its representations of the wilderness/outdoors and imbued with the power to represent nature with all its "sacred meaning and transcendent significance," Dunaway questions their naiveté (2005, xviii). Going a step further, the camera is conceived as a tool that allows the individual users to shape the way they imagine the landscape should be or is. By implication, what the photographer leaves out can arguably have equal significance in defining the landscape and informing environmental debate.

In the documentary film *The River*, which was released in 1937, Pare Lorentz wanted to tell the story of the Mississippi River valley in order to "forge a national identity" while showing the ecological destruction resulting from human impact on the landscape (Dunaway 2005).[10] Conservationists, writers, and planners applauded his "successful" attempt at providing a vision that challenged the government to "fuse nature and technology" in order to merge "the American people with their land" (62). But Lorentz's success was twofold: he also "created a bleached vision of American society, a culture united not only by its landscape but also by its whiteness" (63). While explicitly illustrating the connection between "the organic past of nature and the engineered world of tomorrow," Lorentz refused to acknowledge the "problems of segregation and injustice" and "the crushing poverty of African Americans" (82). Furthermore, he did not address the displacement of black sharecroppers or the legacy of slavery and lynching. According to Dunaway, the film reinforced "the exclusionary vision of the film" that only certain human experiences of the American landscape are relevant and valued (83).

Lorentz's view of the nature-society relationship in the United States made invisible the African American presence on the landscape in direct contrast to media representations of Katrina that largely focused on singular aspects of the African American experience. Both examples demonstrate the power that images have to shape our notions of identity, inclusion, and relationship to place. In the case of Katrina, the images of African Americans were largely confined to that of victim or villain. For the film

The River, black people's lives in relation to their environment were rendered invisible.

National magazines are one format by which the dominant environmental narrative in the United States is transmitted to the public. In particular, magazines that deal explicitly with environmental issues have the power to inform environmental debates, create an "outdoor leisure identity," and provide general information to the masses (Martin 2004, 528). One such publication is *Outside* magazine. Started in 1978, *Outside* declared itself "dedicated to covering the people, sports and activities, politics, art, literature, and hardware of the outdoors" (http://www.outsideonline .com/). True to its word, *Outside* provides stories on a monthly basis that span everything from environmental protests to fluff pieces about what one should wear while camping. I looked at forty-four issues over a ten-year period (1991–2001) using stratified random sampling, in order to get a sense of who it was that *Outside* privileged in their photographs, both in advertisements and straight stories.[11] Stratified random sampling was used in order to include issues from each season (winter, spring, summer, fall). Results show that out of a total of 6,986 pictures, 4,602 pictures contained people. But only 103 pictures of people were African Americans, mostly well-known male sports figures in urban settings (primarily in advertisements).

While *Outside* places white men (and to a lesser degree white women) in diverse outdoors settings around the world, African Americans are limited to landscapes that suggest a fixed identity—at once familiar, common, and narrowly defined. The majority of the pictures of African Americans were black males participating in sports activities, primarily running or basketball, in an urban setting. In addition, most of these pictures featuring African Americans were advertisements for athletic shoes, clothing, or automobiles and featured the faces of well-known sports figures, including Michael Jordan, Carl Lewis, and Patrick Ewing. There were almost no black females, save for track athletes Jackie Joyner Kersee and Florence Griffith Joyner. One vivid exception to the typical black sports figure was the use of world champion bull rider Charlie Sampson. There was a full-page photo of his face, wearing a cowboy hat and showing off his Timex watch.[12]

More recently, this concern seems to have gained some traction at *Outside*. In the July 2011 issue, an article entitled "What's Right with This Picture?" highlights the perspectives of five people of color who are actively involved in environmental issues. The magazine posed the question, why aren't there more people of color enjoying the outdoors? While the racially and ethnically diverse panel shared multiple explanations—the lack or difficulty of access, economic concerns, and a complicated history—the conversation zeroed in on the role of representation in informing the participation of people of color in all things environmental. "People of color don't see themselves in the picture," says Audrey Peterman, who was interviewed for the piece in *Outside*. The result is a misperception that nonwhite people are simply not interested (Peterman 2011, 88).[13]

Some scholars have argued that there is a racialized outdoor leisure identity that is particularly apparent in the advertising industry. In a content analysis of more than four thousand advertisements, Martin (2004) concludes that "Black models are confined to urban and suburban environments while Whites have exclusive domain over the Great Outdoors" (513). His findings, consistent with the analysis in *Outside*, suggest there are potential consequences for how African Americans perceive and participate in outdoor leisure activities.

Many of the interviewees with whom I spoke were frustrated with the scarcity of images of African Americans in nature. When asked to recall images that they have seen of black people in outdoor settings, many respondents could not remember any images of black women outside or only images that showed a black person working. Anita McGruder, who works for the City of Miami, concurs. She comments on seeing male football and basketball stars, but says she "never saw any images of black people skiing," for example.[14] Kris Smith, another Miami resident, sums it up: "There has not been an accurate portrayal of African Americans' relationship with nature."[15] While some respondents might dismiss the issue, saying, "Well, you just *don't* see a lot of black people doing different outdoor activities," others put this down to a type of brainwashing. "A lot of blacks believe phenomena that have been perpetrated on them by the media," says another interviewee.[16]

One interviewee spoke of the resistance of another major magazine, *National Geographic*, to publishing his story. From 1971 until 1993, John Francis walked across the United States to raise environmental awareness. For seventeen of these years he did it without talking. Francis, a United Nations Environment Programme (UNEP) goodwill ambassador, with a doctorate from the University of Wisconsin–Madison, and one of the architects of the Oil Pollution Act of 1990, was initially approached by a member of the *National Geographic* staff to have his story featured in their magazine. In his words, the board decided they would not let a "crazy black person" write a story for *National Geographic*.[17] While his story was eventually published in

an abbreviated fashion in the "Almanac" section at the back of the magazine, he also received an apology from another *National Geographic* fellow
for the board's behavior. For John Francis, the underlying message was not
that he was "crazy," but that he was black.[18] *National Geographic* has published numerous stories of individuals who have walked, ridden, flown, and
sailed over different parts of the world. The only thing that Francis could
see that was different was the color of his skin and that he did not represent
the "norm" of the American environmentalist.[19]

Advertisers and manufacturers can also be blind to African American
experiences in nature settings. The National Black Brotherhood of Skiers
is one of the oldest and the largest (black or white) ski organizations in the
country with a membership totaling more than fourteen thousand people. However, according to one spokesman, while African Americans are
spending millions every year on skiing, it is not reflected in advertisements
(Coleman 1996). According to Bill Simmons, president of a Florida chapter,
"We're not there, but we're there."[20] While African Americans participate in
a wide range of outdoor activities, our media visibility appears to be limited
to work and recreational images that do not consider African Americans'
diversity of experience. As another interviewee put it, "we only see the lawn
man."[21]

It has been suggested that black publications, such as *Essence* magazine,
which targets primarily African American women, need to "step up to the
plate."[22] While *Essence* published an article in 2004 touting the rewards of
spending time with one's children in the outdoors, many interviewees felt
that there is great potential for black publications to do more in addressing
issues relating to the environment.[23] From its inception in 1945, *Ebony*, another national magazine that targets primarily African Americans, carried
articles on the national parks, beaches, and campgrounds where African
Americans could spend their summer vacations.[24] While the motivation
was largely to provide information on safe havens during the era of Jim
Crow, *Ebony* also managed to nurture the environmental imaginations of a
significant proportion of the black population by providing images and stories of African Americans participating in outdoor recreation. But a recent
study on the presence of blacks in advertisements that featured wilderness
settings revealed that *Ebony* may have changed. Compared to *Time* and
Outside, *Ebony* had the lowest number of advertisements featuring African Americans in the outdoors (Martin 2004). This finding suggests that
there is a potential connection between the lack of stories and images in
Ebony about the national parks and other outdoor locations and the low

attendance to national parks today. What people do not see makes it more challenging for them to imagine.

THE NATIONAL PARK SERVICE

In terms of visual representation, the National Park Service (NPS) does not do much better at presenting African Americans participating in diverse environmental activities. In its defense, however, NPS does not exist apart from the prevailing regime of representation. The individuals who work at the NPS are also influenced by the representations in magazines and the ideology that these representations perpetuate. Consequently, the NPS has also been challenged to present African Americans' images and stories within the context of the parks.

A review of the brochures (1991–2001) from three national parks in Florida (Everglades, Biscayne, Big Cypress) revealed that African Americans do not figure prominently in any of them and in most cases, not at all.[25] Brochures of Everglades National Park initially emphasized wilderness, then eventually added people, but they were all white. In a 1991 brochure, while there was a cover photo with six white people, the pamphlet focused primarily on pictures of flora and fauna. From 1992 to the present, there has been a greater focus on people. However, all the photos are of white people participating in outdoor activities (though in some cases, there would be a photo in shadow making it difficult to determine the ethnicity of the individual). A selective review of brochures printed before 1991 had similar results.

For the same period, Biscayne National Park's brochures had only one picture of people—some white snorkelers—among eighteen photos. Biscayne's content was better; the brochure speaks briefly about Native Americans, tree cutters from the Bahamas, pirates, and early settlers. Big Cypress National Park's brochure had no pictures of people and has not changed since 1980. It focuses solely on wildlife, although it mentions Seminole and the Miccosoukee tribes and loggers.

When asked if there were African Americans and other minorities represented in the literature and exhibits, 48 percent of National Park staff at these three parks (who were predominately white) felt that few or no African Americans or other minorities were represented.[26] The primary exception was representation of the Miccosoukee Indians at Big Cypress. Nearly 70 percent felt that there was room for greater minority representation. But only 22 percent of these staff members viewed media representation as a major motivator for greater African American participation. While arguably all three parks possess different specific objectives that reflect their unique landscapes and histories, all three are accessible to the same constituencies in Miami-Dade and Broward Counties. While many staff members felt that funding was the problem, for others it appeared to have more to do with beliefs and perceptions. Using a questionnaire where participants could remain anonymous, staff members were asked, "Are African Americans and/or other minorities represented in park literature and exhibits pertaining to the park? If so how?" One staff member responded, "If a minority group is part of the park story, then they should be represented. If not, don't make up a story." A follow-up question was posed: Do you see room for greater minority representation in park literature and exhibits? This response was more revealing: "Why? Do we change our story?"

For other NPS staff who were asked about the possibility of increasing African American representation in park literature and exhibits and the potential of greater representation attracting more African Americans, there was mixed response. While 70 percent felt there was room for greater representation, only 22 percent identified representation as a key issue for increasing African American participation. This contrasts sharply with the response of African Americans (NPS employees and other environmental professionals) to the same questions, where 46 percent stated that visual and textual representation was needed to increase black participation in the NPS and environmental issues in general. Others felt the need to see more people in the NPS national magazines. "People would appreciate seeing brown faces and olive-toned skin" in park exhibits, says Carole Daniels, NPS research coordinator.[27] Others agree and say they are trying to update exhibits and "tell a more comprehensive story."[28]

While park brochures are slow to reflect the diverse population of the residents who live in Miami-Dade and Broward Counties, a number of initiatives seek to remedy this issue in regard to interpretive exhibits and the park's focus. Shackel (2003) notes that "in 1970, the NPS initiated a program to designate important sites related to African Americans as National Historic Landmarks" (15). In recent years, additional projects focusing on African Americans' experience have come into being. This includes the African American Experience Fund and the Underground Railroad. Quoting an oft-used phrase, black park ranger Shelton Johnson repeats that "A picture's worth a thousand words," when talking about his ongoing project to bring the buffalo soldiers to life at Yosemite National Park.[29] In 1899, the 24th Mounted Infantry, an African American army regiment, was entrusted with the protection of Yosemite, Sequoia, and Kings Canyon National Parks in California. For a long time people forgot their presence in the parks' history, until Shelton Johnson found a picture. In an eloquent letter to the buffalo soldiers, Johnson points to the importance of honoring their memory in the American story. The following is an excerpt from that letter appearing on the website www.shadowsoldier.org:

> You are more than just soldiers of the Twenty-fourth Regiment of Infantry, and this story is bigger than just a chapter in Yosemite's military history. To consider it solely on that level would serve only to diminish your lives and the complexities of the country you lived in. Somehow we have met before. The face of history is never a stranger. The deeper we gaze into the past, the greater our recognition of ourselves in other places and other times. We are all *amnesiacs* stumbling around the world trying to find out who we are, where we belong, and where we come from, until that moment when we find a story that tells us everything about ourselves.

One park in Florida is exploring ways to increase the representation of African American stories and images in their interpretive exhibits and other materials promoting the park. Biscayne National Park (which became part of the park system in 1980), and specifically park ranger Brenda Lanzendorf, sought to make the land on which a black family lived for more than fifty years a National Historic Site.[30] The homesite of Israel Lafayette Jones, fondly referred to as Parson Jones, and his family will tell the story of a man and his family and how they cared for the land and influenced the Miami community.[31] What is particularly stunning about the story is the context of when and how the Jones family came to prominence.

In the early twentieth century, the United States was experiencing racial tensions that arose from the emancipation of thousands of enslaved Africans. While many northern black people experienced a circumscribed freedom, many in the southern states still struggled with de facto enslavement or feared reenslavement. In addition, white supremacists erected further barriers that constrained African Americans determined to build a new life. Black people were denied the right to vote, barred from frequenting white business establishments and educational institutions, and forbidden to hold religious services without the presence of a licensed white minister (Earle 2000).

Florida was no exception. The majority of black people who lived in what is now Dade County were former runaway slaves and Bahamian refugees (Dunn 1997). Few possessed the means to establish a homestead and run a successful business. It is within this context that Israel Lafayette Jones traveled from North Carolina to Florida, further developed agricultural and maritime skills, and successfully produced pineapples and limes on his own farm. In addition, he expanded his wealth through real estate and played an integral role in the development of the black community in Dade County.

Born in 1858 in Raleigh, North Carolina, Jones became a major fixture on the social landscape as a farmer, philosopher, and preacher. He had two sons with his wife, Moselle Albury. King Arthur Lafayette Jones was born in March of 1897, and their second son, Sir Lancelot Garfield Jones, was born a year and a half later in October of 1898.[32] The two boys are believed to be the first black Americans born on Key Biscayne.[33] The Jones family made significant contributions socially and financially to the Miami-Dade community, and the Jones farm became one of the largest producers of pineapples and limes on the east coast of Florida using unusual agricultural practices. But they will probably be remembered most for their contribution to the National Park system.[34] Starting in 1961 and continuing throughout the decade of the 1960s, a harsh political battle ensued between competing investors who incorporated the city of Islandia and hoped to develop the islands (Bennett 2002). Islandia was Miami-Dade County's smallest municipality, comprised of a chain of thirty-two islands that included the Jones's property.[35] Lancelot and Arthur were the second largest property owners within Islandia.[36] In addition, they were the only permanent year-long residents from north Key Largo to Soldier Key. By 1985, only one other private citizen aside from Lancelot Jones lived within the boundaries of Islandia along with the resident park rangers. Lancelot would share his ecological knowledge, particularly about sponges, with all who would listen, including school children who visited the nearby Adams Key Ranger Station's Environmental Education Center. The sponge industry was a subject particularly close to Lancelot's heart and important to the environmental history of the region. In 1890, hundreds of fishermen—Cuban, American, and Bahamian—depended upon commercial sponge fishing for their livelihoods.[37]

In 1968, the area was declared a National Monument and in 1980, it was declared a National Park. Motivated by the belief that the area should be preserved, Lancelot and his sister-in-law Kathleen sold their share of the island to the National Park Service in 1970.[38] The National Park Service paid them $1.2 million for a parcel consisting of more than 277 acres. Lancelot Jones was granted the right to live out his remaining years in the family home.

This story has resonated with many Miami residents. Numerous photos of the site and interviews with photos of Lancelot Jones, concerned African American citizens, and local park staff have appeared in newspapers throughout Miami-Dade County for the last ten years. In addition, a local community group called Miami Community Partners, comprised primarily of African Americans, is using the Jones story as one vehicle to get more African Americans interested in recapturing the history of their community and the parks. As a result of the groundswell of interest and support for the Jones site, the African American community in Miami-Dade County has been inspired to participate in management of the site.[39]

While the NPS is arguably making strides in creating more inclusive narratives within its interpretive exhibits and other park materials, many feel that it still has a long way to go.[40] In 1999, a Mosaic conference (a diverse gathering of people of color concerned with environmental issues) was held to address barriers, real and perceived, that prevent African Americans and all people of color from seeing the parks as their own and as part of a collective ownership and entitlement (U.S. Department of the Interior 2000). New NPS units that focus on African American history links to national parks and historic sites include the Cane River National Historic Site (NHS), Tuskegee Airmen NHS, and Martin Luther King Jr. Memorial. But some question the extent to which NPS explores histories that have previously been marginalized and neglected. In a study that was done at Arlington House, Robert E. Lee National Monument, visitors and staff were asked about their point of view regarding how slavery and race were presented at the site. While some lauded the attempt of NPS to address slavery, many felt that the story was underemphasized, and all of the visitors surveyed felt they did not learn anything new about race or slavery (Strait 2004). The researcher concluded that there is a need for the history of under-represented subjects to be "retold in full and equal detail" (17).

Like the NPS, other environmental institutions and organizations are vulnerable to the power of representations affecting the way they promote their cause while asking for greater participation from diverse constituencies. One case in point is the American Hiking Society. This organization emphasizes volunteer trail work and fun as part of the experience it offers. However, on their website, all the pictures of white people showed them relaxing while the one picture of a black person was shown working.

The people who created the site did not see anything wrong until a black woman, who was hired to help them address the lack of diversity in their membership, pointed it out to them.[41] Sid Wilson, president of Private Guide, Inc., in Denver, experienced something similar. He described a story that appeared in the Sunday supplement of the newspaper a few years ago. The story spoke about a group of kids learning how to climb, explicitly geared toward attracting a diverse audience. The photo was of a black girl on a belay, but she was crying and clearly not having any fun. Wilson just shook his head and said, "How was that going to get black folks interested?"[42] The use of this image suggests a lack of understanding about the underlying meanings of images and how they resonate with African Americans. According to Wilson, "they [white people] don't want to put our face on things."

SEEING IS BELIEVING

The impact of the limited representation of African Americans in the outdoors is expressed in various ways. At Vanderbilt University in Tennessee, a female African American student spoke about her frustration with some of her black friends and classmates who do not recycle because "that's for white people."[43] This was a sentiment echoed by many of the African Americans interviewed for this research, who hold professional and leadership positions in environmental organizations. You know how the saying goes, spoke one interviewee, "The worst thing you can be is country."[44] Price Cobbs, psychologist and coauthor of *Black Rage*, addresses the question of agency by asking if black people have "shrunk our ledge" and led ourselves to believe that we are limited in what we can understand, how we interpret what it means to be authentically black, and what we feel our voices should be lent to (Grier and Cobbs 1968). Cobbs asks, "Do you collide with the ledge? Do you write about something non-black, like French cinema, and broaden the ledge?" (92). Systemic and institutional processes notwithstanding (see Chapter 5), one decides what one does and does not do if one is to be "authentically" black. This belief is partially driven by a desire of African Americans to challenge historical definitions that have hijacked black identity, and to redefine black identity on their own terms (Klotman and Cutler 1999). Authenticity, in this sense, is partially defined by resistance to depictions of black identity that lack complexity and are demeaning. But in an effort by African Americans to maintain "membership" in the black community by solidifying a definition of blackness that resists negative images and professes pride, there is a danger of limiting one's possibilities in much the same way that negative representations have done. Defining black identity becomes less about expanding our possibilities and more about not being perceived as trying to be white by doing "white" activities (e.g., recycling).

Others feel that it is a lack of awareness of the possibilities that have kept many black people from imagining themselves in a more expansive manner relating to the environment. Fifty-two percent of those interviewed who work for environmental organizations believe that an increase in the positive representation of African Americans in relation to environmental issues offers a chance to expand awareness and ultimately participation by the African American community. "The image of the African American has always been the slave-type, field work, [doing] work that's undesirable," lamented one interviewee.[45] While some African Americans manage to "turn off commercialized visions" of how black people are imagined, still others grow angry that they "won't see a grandmother, mother in open space."[46] There is a paucity of imagery that highlights black folks creatively and positively interacting with their natural environment, be it hiking or working in an urban garden.

Thirty-seven percent of black residents and professionals surveyed nationally and in Dade County cited lack of awareness as the number one reason why black people do not participate in environmental activities, and 67 percent listed it among their top three reasons. Interviewees were given eight potential choices to choose from: economics, exclusionary practices, fear, lack of awareness, lack of access/mobility, lack of interest, stigma associated with slavery and agriculture, and other (a category for them to fill in). When asked to comment on their choices, interviewees spoke about how people do not know about opportunities (no one is telling them); do not know about connections between civic involvement in resource management activities and the benefits to be accrued in their daily lives (lack of ownership, lack of power in decision-making positions, mistrust in those black gatekeepers who may not be voicing the concerns of the community); and don't believe it has anything to do with who they are, particularly as black people. Increased media representation that emphasizes the "black experience" is integral to increasing awareness and attracting black participation. For some, equating greater media representation to increased environmental participation is based on the notion that it helps when you "see yourself reflected in the imagery."[47] For others, it comes down to "media-specific marketing" that specifically targets African Americans.[48]

Their comments included: "It seems like everyone else is the expert," and "No one took the time to engage us in the conservation movement."

In addition to a lack of visual representations to stir the imaginations of potential black resource users, interviewees bemoaned the lack of recognition of black people doing environmental work. There is a need for greater recognition of the existing network of black environmentalists and an ongoing acknowledgement of black stories that aren't only told within the usual framework of the white context/gaze featured only during Black History month.

MaVynee Betsch is one such African American environmentalist who after years of work to preserve and protect both the natural and cultural history of American Beach, had begun to find some representational prominence in mainstream media, most recently on the cover of *Preservation* magazine.[49] Betsch, who donated her significant wealth to environmental causes and succeeded in convincing the NPS to bring 8.2 acres of sand dunes under their protection, spent more than twenty years doing environmental work, ultimately bringing attention to environmental issues in her community. But the larger environmental community resisted using her as a poster child.

MaVynee Betsch and John Francis challenge the representational norms within the mainstream environmental movement. The choice *not* to use either as poster people for the environment is indicative of something more than happenstance. While Julia Butterfly Hill[50] is symbolic of the persistence and possibility associated with youth, Betsch and Francis—both older and black—as one white environmentalist admitted to me at a workshop—"challenges our comfort zones."[51] He went on to speak about how Betsch and Francis live their lives according to their environmental values from "balls to bones" and by their very presence, actively challenge others to do the same. Julia Butterfly Hill, on the other hand, can be dismissed because of her youth.

African Americans are negotiating these historical practices of representation in creative ways. Some are challenging existing frameworks through nonprofit organizations. After twenty years of working in various capacities within the environmental movement, Iantha Gantt-Wright decided to start her own organization, the Kenian Group, a consulting organization that provides training, conference planning, and facilitation for environmental groups that are interested in diversity issues. She is adamant when speaking about any organization truly desiring change. "You cannot build the foundation of your house, organization, and then make diversity something you put in afterwards, like windows or doors."[52] She also emphasizes the need to see more African Americans in environmental organizations' magazines.

Others are creating their own media outlets, such as Earthwise Productions, run by Audrey Peterman. Recognized by the National Parks and Conservation Organization (she is on their board and has been given numerous awards), Peterman works to engage African Americans in environmentalism, outdoor recreation, and the protection of national parks in the United States. The focus of the organization is threefold: provide consultancy services to mainstream environmental organizations who are looking to diversify their membership base, coordinate tours of the national parks to encourage more African Americans to utilize their national parks and forests, and publish a monthly newsletter that promotes a comprehensive view of the environment.[53]

There are also black individuals working within the park service to engineer change. These include the aforementioned park ranger Shelton Johnson who is making the buffalo soldier's story integral to the narrative of Yosemite through interpretive exhibits, websites, and live reenactments. Carla Cowles focuses on the historical interpretations of park sites that have explicit African American experiences embedded in the landscape. She works on "changing the way people look at history" and the way people look at others.[54]

There are also writers, artists, and photographers who are interested in expanding our perception of black people in relationship to the environment. Eddy Harris, a self-proclaimed black outdoorsman, has published a number of books on his backwoods experiences, most notably *Mississippi Solo*, a memoir of his travels down the Mississippi by canoe. For Harris, revelations about the mighty Mississippi were intertwined with insights about himself as a black man in America. When asked about how he defines "environment," Harris stated firmly that the definition of environment "changes depending on where in the landscape the black guy is."[55] A similar understanding of how place and black identity mutually inform each other is expressed by nature photographer Dudley Edmondson who completed a book that focuses on black people's experiences in wild places.[56] Inspired by his concern over the lack of African American faces in the wilderness areas he worked in, he interviewed African Americans who had a variety of environmental backgrounds. Edmondson came to the conclusion that you could not talk about nature and African Americans without addressing "slavery, racial prejudice and personal safety." For people of color, "these issues are very real and are crucial to their participation in the outdoors" (Edmondson 2006, 6).

While some use the pen to get their message across, others use the paintbrush. Artists such as Gary Moore create public outdoor work that reflects the African American experience. Based in Miami, Moore integrates paintings depicting black history with trees and other elements of the natural environment in outdoor public spaces. "The whole environmental movement is looked at as one of the white-isms, something white people do," states Moore.[57] By creating art in public spaces that explicitly celebrates African American history in relation to the environment, Moore feels we can explore and remember the "nostalgia that black people have for the earth." Others, such as the Highwaymen, continue to bring their paintings of the Floridian landscape to the public.[58] While their paintings of the natural environment rarely contained a human element, one painter acknowledged how "your background goes into the painting."[59] Another artist concurs; he sees the work as an "expression of you on canvas." While "the Highwaymen are an enigma in the course of American Art history because African Americans are not supposed to be painting the kind of landscape we're painting," most pushed ahead and provided stunning expressions of the Florida landscape that continue to excite the imagination.

Each of these individuals was partly motivated by the need to see his or her own experience of the natural environment expressed in such a way that it invites others to reconsider how the multiple aspects of our identities influence our environmental perspective. As African Americans, they offer alternatives to the limited representations of black people in nature put forth by the mainstream media. For many of the artists that I interviewed, these alternatives are sorely needed to engage more African Americans in environmental participation. As one interviewee put it, "I tend to turn off commercialized visions. . . . I tend to reject that as my reality."[60]

CONCLUSION

In this chapter, I examined how the lack of visual and textual representation of African Americans in popular media and the national parks perpetuates the invisibility of African Americans in conversations about environmental management. I highlighted how African American concerns and interests in relation to the environment have not been articulated, invited, or understood in the accepted context of the environmental movement and natural resource management. As a consequence, the idea of a "white wilderness" is perpetuated, and African Americans are intentionally or unintentionally excluded.

It is the dichotomy between media images of African Americans in the outdoors/environment (either the lack of or stereotypes) and the reality of black representation in outdoor activities and other environmental concerns that created a space to explore the "politics of visual representation, and the dismantling of the myth of a monolithic African American community" (Walker 1994, 69). Cultural memories can be suppressed or awakened by media representations and create the potential of increasing African American environmental participation. Findings suggest that the lack of visual and textual representation (i.e., stories about black experience and images of African Americans engaged with the natural environment) shapes some of the negative attitudes blacks have about the environment and that whites hold about African American environmental attitudes. Conversely, narratives that include and/or privilege an African American experience invite greater African American participation in governing and enjoying public parks, forests, and green spaces. For the majority of African Americans I interviewed for this research, "environment" was defined in one of two ways: as something distant, outside their purview, and largely white *or* as something local, close to home, and reflecting their own experience. For African American environmental and community leaders, drawing explicit connections between an individual's or community's identity and how they interact with their natural environment through media representations is a sure-fire way to increase African American environmental interaction. While environmental organizations such as the NPS are actively seeking ways to increase African American interest and participation in using and managing the parks, there seems to be a gap in understanding the power of stories and imagery to create a more inclusive vision of the park as a place representing a wide array of American experience.

On a more general note, environmental organizations need to find ways of incorporating African American historical images in political, social, and environmental memory. As one interviewee put it, "we are so limited in our perceptions of the environment."[61] Truncated, abbreviated, or singular, historical accounts being touted as the "official history" of a place rob us of the opportunity, and deny us the possibility, of knowing who we are, as part of an American collective identity. Specifically, these representations deny all people the possibility of working together toward a vision of environmental management that embraces the needs and priorities of our communities with understanding and creativity.

CHAPTER FIVE

It's Not Easy Being Green

Black people have a complicated relationship with America. For us, it's painful love. It has an old history filled with slavery and Jim Crow, so to love America requires a lot more of us.

—Dr. Blair Kelley, quoted in Touré, *Who's Afraid of Post-Blackness?*

I outgrew my rage, but retained my passion.

—Betty Reid Soskin, the oldest park ranger in the National Park Service

On a warm, autumn day in October of 2005, approximately eighty individuals assembled to spend three days at the Summit 2005 conference on "Diverse Partners for Environmental Progress" in Wakefield, Virginia. This historic conversation connected leaders from various environmental, community, and national organizations and movements to "develop a common framework that supports a pro-environment slate of issues" ("Steps for the Future" 2005). An ethnically and racially diverse group (people of color appeared to outnumber European Americans), they ranged from academics to environmental justice supporters, nonprofit groups, and representatives and leaders from the National Park Service, the Trust for Public Lands, and the civil rights movement. One of the primary goals of this three-day workshop was to discuss the "real and perceived" barriers to more effective collaborative efforts between those within the mainstream environmental movement and those who occupy the borders. While some consensus emerged around a few issues, such as the discrepancy in financial resources available to major environmental organizations compared with small nonprofits and the role of power in decision-making processes, the subject that seemed to garner the greatest consensus was that racism is a significant barrier to greater collaborative success in meeting the needs and concerns of environmentalists of color and their constituents. African American and Native American participants were particularly vocal on this subject, with many echoing the sentiment that, indeed, it's not easy being green.

Whether spoken or unspoken, this is the same conclusion that many African Americans come to, and it is arguably the issue most deeply embedded, highly contested, and emotionally charged. Yet a clear understanding of what racism is or agreement on how it is articulated institutionally or individually is not always apparent. Racism is also hotly debated in part because of the difficulty in arriving at a consensus on the "explanations and potential remedies" (Frazier, Margai, and Tettie-Fio 2003, 55).

In this chapter, I discuss how racism and diversity are two hot-button topics that people seem to embrace or reject, but which arise either implicitly or explicitly in the "environment" conversation.[1] How is African American participation perceived by environmental organizations, and how do African Americans actually experience the natural environment and the organizations that manage it? I will discuss the challenges that racism and diversity present to African Americans and mainstream environmental organizations that are interested in creating more inclusive contexts in which diverse individuals and communities can enter into environmental management. In addition, I will discuss some of the debates on racism and diversity and present findings that highlight the frustrations and concerns of African American professionals and leaders who struggle to develop strategies that effectively deal with racism in practical ways within decision-making contexts. Finally, I will argue that there is a general disconnect between African American environmental professionals and their white counterparts regarding the perception of exclusion and racism within an environmental context.

RACISM IN BLACK AND WHITE

In *The Dictionary of Human Geography*, racism is defined as "an ideology of difference whereby social significance is attributed to culturally constructed categories of race" (Jackson 1994, 496). While academic and concise, this definition belies the emotional nature of racism as well as its consequences. According to scholar-activist Ron Daniels, racism is not just individual acts perpetrated on one person by another. "Historically, racism constituted and constitutes a system of special privileges, benefits, and psychological and symbolic and material rewards for white people" (2002, 1). Racism is systemic—it is embedded in our institutions and our way of life. Racism is not the same as prejudice. While black people may have prejudicial feelings toward white people, these feelings "are in no way linked to a system of domination that affords [black people] any power to coercively control the lives and well-being of white folks" (hooks 1992, 15). Whether it is the ability of some to translate their prejudices into institutional practices that have macro-scale material affects or the impact of ideology influenced by our everyday practices of using language and images whose meanings are inherently divisive (e.g., black lie vs. white lie, black sheep of the family, black Monday), racism is a process that at best limits opportunities and stifles potential collaborative efforts and at worst creates a negative space of hatred and mistrust that can lead to violence and even death (Daniels 2002).[2]

Some activists and scholars argue that the ultimate goal for many African Americans is not "so much integration and assimilation," but instead, equity and equality (Daniels 2002, 17). To this end, Daniels argues, emphasis should be placed on systematic and scientific programs that focus on eliminating racism through individual and institutional efforts. Within an environmental context, how do we analyze, interpret, understand, and articulate a phenomenon that is real for many, nonexistent for others, but affects everyone? African Americans working in nongovernmental organizations and community groups have been actively taking on this challenge for years. The environmental justice movement emerged in the 1980s as a vehicle for addressing social justice concerns and taking on the question of racism (Gelobter et al. 2005). One of the core "environmental justice principles" set forth at the first People of Color Leadership Summit in 1991 explicitly addresses this issue:

> The Principles of Working Together require affirmation of the value
> of diversity and the rejection of any form of racism, discrimination,
> and oppression. To support each other completely, we must learn
> about our different cultural and political histories so that we can
> completely support each other in our movement inclusive of ages,
> classes, immigrants, indigenous peoples, undocumented workers,
> farm workers, genders, sexual orientations and education differ-
> ences. (Principles of Working Together Working Group 2002, 1–2)

But twenty years later, the mainstream environmental movement is accused of falling short of addressing certain concerns, such as managing to "racially integrate their senior staff" (Gelobter et al. 2005). While not citing "overt discrimination" as the reason, environmental justice advocates believe that their goals of social justice are not fully embraced as priorities. "The mainstream environmental movement . . . remains largely white, and environmental organizations still work on issues most relevant to the white communities" (Merchant 2003, 390).[3]

In addition, one has to first acknowledge that racism exists before one can explain it and pursue practical solutions. For many white Americans, admission of racism implies personal responsibility and the possibility that they are racist. In addition, the "obliteration of the black past" from the meta-narrative of America allows for the rationalization of racism and the continuation of white domination (Marable 2006, 20). Manning Marable, a professor of history, political science, and public policy at Columbia (who passed away in 2011), put it this way:

> Since "race" is a fraudulent concept, devoid of scientific reality, "racism" can only be rationalized and justified through suppression of black counternarratives that challenge society's understanding about itself and its own past. Racism is perpetuated and reinforced by the "historical logic of whiteness," which repeatedly presents whites as the primary (and frequently sole) actors in the important decisions that have influenced the course of human events. This kind of history deliberately excludes blacks and other racialized groups from having the capacity to become actors in shaping major outcomes.

Ellis Cose, in his qualitative work on the rage of the black middle class, highlighted how, regardless of class differences, blacks and whites "live fundamentally different lives" (1993, 4). Consequently, even for those who work together in the same institutions, it is impossible to imagine the world from the other's perspective. Specifically, it becomes difficult for whites to understand the "soul-destroying slights" and discrimination experienced by their black counterparts (5). Besides, the framework used by both liberals and conservatives to discuss race "leaves us intellectually debilitated, morally disempowered, and personally depressed" (C. West 2001, 4). As a result, African Americans find themselves frustrated and fatigued and having to defend themselves against charges that they are "playing the race card."

Regardless of the challenges, "the problem of the twenty-first century remains the problem of the color line" (C. West 2001, xiv). Racism spawns internalized and lateral oppression, inequality, meanness, denial, and hatred. For African Americans, the vestiges of white supremacy have meant a loss of self-love and a lived experience that "yields black nihilism" (xviii). Within an environmental context, it can exclude people from participating in decision-making processes and having access to resources, which has real economic, social, and spiritual consequences. But while the consequences of racism can be laid bare, coming up with practical solutions is not so easy. Within the context of this research, what is most problematic is getting everyone concerned to agree that there is a problem in the first place.

Race is a "constitutive feature of modern power and a formative prism in shaping lived experience" (Moore, Kosek, and Pandian 2003). In the final analysis, it may be that the important point is not whether or not racism exists. Instead, focus should be placed on how the "perception of race" and in turn, the perception of racism, expresses itself (Holland 2002). If race is thought to be an important determinant for the individual or a community, then it needs to be seriously considered. This entails engaging black people's experience in order to get an idea "of what it's like to be black in a predominately white society" (Sibley 1995, 146). In W. E. B. Du Bois's important work on social space within an urban context, *The Philadelphia Negro*, he offered observations on segregation that white academics had not done, by centering his study on black people's experiences (Sibley 1995; Du Bois 1995). Other studies on similar subjects reflected "the remote, universalizing view of spatial science which does not engage with people's experience and, thus, has nothing to say about contrasting world-views, and problems like racism" (Sibley 1995, 147).

One general solution to addressing racism has been to promote diversity in order to reflect the changing multicultural demographics in the United States. Advocates for diversity policies in academic, political, and environmental institutions discuss the need to shift the balance of power and divert any impulse to marginalize an individual or community because of racial difference. By encouraging diversity within our institutions and corporations, some people reason, racism cannot help but be vanquished through the experience of working and learning with others different from ourselves. While the premise on which diversity is based is often applauded, the methods by which it is achieved are, in contrast, furiously challenged by those who instead see quotas and preferences that lead to a zero-sum equation (Guinier and Torres 2002). Affirmative action, as a strategy designed to address the "particular struggles and specific demands of the Civil Rights movement," has arguably provoked the greatest amount of furor from its opponents who believe that African Americans are getting preferential treatment over white Americans. Since affirmative action was a response to the civil rights movement, "the central issue . . . was the status of the Negro in American society" (Marable 2006, 207). However, by the year 2000, the majority of those who benefited from affirmative action were *not* African American, but arguably those from other countries.[4]

Similar debates are taking place among coworkers within environmental institutions such as the National Park Service as well as between various institutions and organizations. For some within these institutions, the challenge lies in developing "a more inclusive, culturally sensitive, broad-based environmental agenda that will appeal to many people and unite many sectors of the movement" (Taylor 1997, 16). While there have been strategies implemented that have advanced this goal, for many African Americans working within environmental organizations, it has not been enough. As one long-time NPS park staffer put it, "We have to swim across rivers of denial."[5]

RACISM IN THE UNITED STATES:
Viewpoints from across the Spectrum

A few years ago on C-Span, African American scholar and writer Shelby Steele spoke out against affirmative action and other similar strategies designed to increase the diversity of African Americans in educational institutions as well as corporations. Known publicly as a black conservative, Steele argued that programs like affirmative action only succeeded at making African Americans seem incapable of acquiring jobs or entry into universities on merit alone.[6] In his view, this results in African Americans feeling inadequate and not being considered equals by European Americans. For Steele, the primary problem for black people in the United States is their inability to embrace the responsibilities of freedom and that position's incompatibility with "worshipping at the church of racism."[7]

I argue that this conversation is framed in such a way that masks the complexity of the "black position" on this subject. It is not primarily a polarized view—that you are either Bill Cosby preaching personal responsibility or Jesse Jackson screaming racism. I suggest that the majority of African Americans take a more complex position. They recognize and advocate for their own agency and, indeed, feel it is necessary for them to "not wait for crumbs from the white man's table" as some have phrased it. But they also recognize that they do not experience their agency or freedom in isolation. They do so within a larger context where racism is embedded and is systemic. For all people, the reality and materiality of day-to-day life is largely shaped by the context in which they live. Therefore, to completely turn away from the "church of racism"—to believe that African Americans can fully embrace their "freedom" in this way—is to deny a reality that not only has personal consequences, but relinquishes for everyone the responsibility to change the way things are.

In his acclaimed work *Race Matters*, Cornel West eloquently discusses the two positions that Steele elucidates and finds them both wanting. Liberal structuralists (like Jesse Jackson), emphasize "structural constraints [that] relate almost exclusively to the economy and politics" but do not necessarily look at the "structural character of culture" (C. West 2001, 20). In addition, they may fear that if they talk about culture, which implies addressing values, they will sound too much like conservatives and take attention away from the structural issues. In contrast, conservative behaviorists (like Shelby Steele) "talk about values and attitudes as if political and economic structures hardly exist" (21). Eschewing real social and historical analyses that acknowledge the systemic and structural processes that African Americans encounter, conservative behaviorists appear to ignore the inequality of opportunity and instead stress agency, or "personal responsibility" for not being a victim.

The ability of Americans to exercise freedom is largely dependent on the institutions they become involved in, the government policies that are designed to impose and create order, and the beliefs of the communities in which they live. Freedom does not "happen" within a vacuum. For African Americans, fully exercising freedom entails a shifting or reframing of the issue. Instead of confining a discussion about race "to the problems black people pose for whites," we must "consider what this way of viewing black people reveals about the United States as a nation" (C. West 2001, 5).

TALKING THE TALK, WALKING THE WALK: *Being Green*

There is no monolithic African American environmental experience. While there is arguably a collective experience of living in a country where racism is part of the nation's fabric, the personal experience for each African American (as it would be for anyone) is shaped by economic, generational, and gender differences, the place where you live, your social and educational background, and ultimately, the choices you make.[8] It is important not to confuse or conflate the historical need of African Americans to privilege race in order to address major issues (e.g., segregation) with the belief that all African Americans experience day-to-day life in much the same way.[9] While identifying common themes provides a starting point for deeper discussion, a sweeping generalization of the African American environmental experience obscures the complexity of that experience and therefore derails attempts at effectively addressing specific environmental issues.

I found that people's responses to my questions about the practices of environmental organizations, diversity initiatives, and African American environmental interactions were informed by where they lived (geographical region, rural/suburban/urban status), their economic status, age, and to a lesser degree gender, but the commonalities in their responses outweighed their differences.[10] While it was tempting, for example, to fall back on the rural/urban dichotomy to frame their responses, what became exceedingly clear was that the experience of being black trumped any place-based assertions related to environmental engagement. For many African Americans I spoke with, their economic and mobility status was fluid; they may have grown up on a farm, but lived in a city as an adult. They may have raised their kids in a suburb, but retired to a rural area. But no matter where they found themselves, they were always black. And while the meaning of blackness in all of its complexity and real-life manifestations has arguably shifted over time, the collective historical experience of being black in America has not. These similarities in attitudes and perceptions draw from a collective history and consciousness that is reinforced and remembered through media, textual representation, and experience. "The collective experience of pain and hardship, suffering and sacrifice has given African Americans a unique perspective from which our consciousness has been forged" (Marable 2006, 39). In addition, regardless of where one stands in the race debate, the history of white supremacy in the United States and how it has been articulated on the landscape is difficult to dispute, though some charge that "historical amnesia" does make it easier to deny or forget. (Marable 2006).

For environmental organizations such as the National Park Service, the experience of changing to reflect the diversity of the United States has been one fraught with growing pains. Gentry Davis, who has been with the NPS for almost four decades remembered when he was the only nonwhite person working at Yellowstone Park in the 1970s. He lamented that the NPS was predominately white and male, with a small percentage of white females. Gentry felt that he was not seeing "the face of America."[11] In addition, he believes that top managers feel threatened by minorities in key positions. When African Americans do get in key positions, they are "under that microscope," he says, which has less to do with their capabilities and more to do with white people's beliefs and feelings about black people. "We live in a society where race is the first thing on everyone's mind, but the last thing discussed," remarked another long-time park employee.[12]

An environmental workshop at the Garrison Institute in upstate New York illustrates this point. Forty experienced and in some cases distinguished environmental professionals, academics, and theologians came together for a four-day workshop entitled "Heart and Mind of Environmental Leadership" to evaluate a collaborative project aimed at framing "environmental issues around core American values" (Heart and Mind 2005).[13] Participants included representatives from the Trust for Public Lands, the National Park Service, the Mountain Institute (an international nonprofit focused on the conservation of mountain ecosystems worldwide), and Yale University. Participation was by invitation only. I was fortunate to receive an invitation from a park service employee who had seen me present my research at an earlier conference and thought it would have relevance. During the workshop, this steering committee member confided to me the other reason I was invited—they were having a difficult time coming up with a short list of people of color to invite (I was surprised by this admission). When they did extend invitations to a few people, all declined for various reasons, one that would become clear to me after the workshop.

On the first evening, we gathered in a large circle in a meditation room, watched over by a huge, golden Buddha. The Garrison Institute used to be a monastery, and everything about the design of the building—the modest rooms, high ceilings, emphasis on quiet contemplation, and well-kept courtyards—reminded you of this fact. As we sat around the circle, one thing became very clear. I was the only person of color and, because of my status as a Ph.D. student, one of the least experienced and knowledgeable people in the room. But over the next three days, while discussions about patriotism, values, identity, and connecting with the grassroots movement ensued, I was continually turned to when questions of race or diversity came up. I became the expert; so much so that no one realized, least of all myself, that I was expected primarily to engage only in breakout sessions that had to do with race.[14] On the last day, the tension between my role as race "expert" and desire to participate beyond those limitations came to a breaking point. What followed was an honest and emotional dialogue between me and the other participants on questions about race and the mainstream environmental movement. Some participants admitted to "dropping the ball" when creating a more diverse list of invitees. Others revealed that they were "tired" of having to deal with the issue, but recognized its importance. Most telling was one comment from a well-known voice within the environmental community. He chastised his cohorts and himself by saying that they were all just "too comfortable," and no one was interested in being uncomfortable.

According to many African Americans that I interviewed this anecdotal experience is a reflection of a pattern of behavior within the larger environmental movement that continues. They spoke of the resistance by many to talk about racism, or to provide continued financial support for diversity programs, and about the entrenchment of the "old boys network" within mainstream environmental organizations. While 96 percent of the black environmental professionals I interviewed said that their organizations or institutions had diversity initiatives, 42 percent qualified their answers to express their dissatisfaction with these initiatives. "The problem is, there have been many [such initiatives], said one NPS employee.[15] Another complained that it's just "a lot of lip service about diversity." One man summed it up best when asked if there was a diversity initiative at his institution: "You're looking at him."[16]

Within the NPS a number of strategies and programs have been developed to address issues of diversity in their visitorship, staff, and surrounding communities. These initiatives include youth and social science programs, the National Underground Railroad Network to Freedom and a Workforce Diversity Management Program (Roberts 2004). While these programs have been met with varying degrees of enthusiasm and support, arguably the biggest boost for these initiatives was the appointment of Robert Stanton by President Bill Clinton in 1988. After twenty-five years with the NPS, he became the first African American to serve as director.

When asked how he came to the NPS, Stanton spoke of Stewart Udall, who became secretary of the interior in the early 1960s. Udall noticed that "when he came into the office and looked at the workforce . . . he saw brothers and sisters on the street . . . but he didn't see those faces in the halls of the interior, or in the parks, or within the wildlife refuges."[17] Udall decided to initiate a program where he would personally recruit African Americans from historically black colleges and universities, and Robert Stanton was one of the first African Americans to find himself with a job in the park service. Stanton takes great pride in the fact that under his watch, three African American sites became part of the national parks, including Little Rock Central High School in Arkansas.[18] When asked about the challenges of engaging a black constituency, he underscored something he saw take place time and again within the NPS. "If you say over and over again that

lks don't like parks because they're not in the parks, the park ser-
ople begin to believe that and the black people begin to believe it
lves." Stanton added, "It becomes a self-fulfilling prophecy, to a lot
ple's satisfaction, quite candidly."

BARRIERS: *What's Race Got to Do with It?*

Many of the African Americans I spoke with were frustrated at the resistance and unwillingness of white colleagues to discuss race. One interviewee expressed this sentiment: "Some of us are lullabyed into believing
all is well." But others feel it goes deeper than that. At the 2005 Diverse
Partners for Environmental Progress summit in Wakefield, Virginia ("Steps
for the Future" 2005), participants drew up a list of perceived barriers to
greater collaboration between the largely white environmental movement
and communities of color. The list included:

1. Racism, white privilege, and internalized oppression
2. Different levels of commitment to working together
3. Cultural competency issues
4. Environmental field seen as exclusionary
5. Unequal power and resources; the foundation funding process
6. Education—no youth education; sustainable solutions instead of
   quick fixes
7. Lack of accountability
8. The 1980s "me generation"—a shift from the community to the individual, fragmentation

In relation to comments on racism and white privilege, black and brown
environmentalists revealed their mistrust of white environmental organizations. One summit participant reminded us of William Bennett's comments earlier that year (2005) when he linked the imagined abortion of all
black babies to a drop in crime rate. The participant believed that they were
operating in a climate that supported Bennett's comments. Others spoke
about the "negative space" created by racism—the anger, denial, and frustration that creates a kind of no-fly zone particularly for black ideas among
white people; one's viewpoint will surely get shot down if caught entering this territory. While the group seemed to have no problem at creating
consensus around the major issues, what also became clear at the summit
was how the decision-making process concerning potential strategies was

fraught with tensions between various participants representing different constituencies. Some concern was expressed over how the limited pot of resources would be allocated (particularly concerning the nonprofits), and that specific priorities and needs ought to be addressed more than others.

African Americans mentioned the following concerns:

- Anger and resentment: African American environmental practitioners point to a lack of acknowledgement among their white colleagues about issues of privilege and how that shapes a person's ability to inform the environmental debate. One individual could remember her and her family being chased out of a park in Virginia by the Ku Klux Klan. These memories run deep for African Americans.[19] For white Americans, she felt that forgetting about segregation was a case of "voluntary amnesia."[20] Another expressed uncertainty, suggesting that this lack of knowledge in the park service "could be racism." Others felt that there were different levels of commitment to working together, issues of differing cultural competency, and concerns that the environmental field can be exclusionary because of its attitudes, assumptions, use of language, and clubbyness. At the Summit 2005, anger and resentment were evident by the emotional retorts and overall exasperation about these issues. As one woman put it, "I've been talking about this for years."
- Denial and defensiveness: There is a chasm in understanding between the answers of white NPS employees and black and non-NPS employees. When asked what they thought were the most important issues concerning African American environmental interaction, 35 percent of the white NPS employees simply did not answer. For those who did answer, 17 percent chose "lack of interest." About 35 percent of park staff listed "exclusionary practices" as the *least* important issue. Forty-three percent listed it as a *nonissue*. Thirteen percent listed "exclusionary practices" somewhere between their second and their sixth choice. One individual felt the need to question the inclusion of "exclusionary practices" as an option. "What? Are you kidding? Where does this idea come from?"

The response from African Americans was quite different. Thirty-five percent of African Americans listed "exclusionary practices" in their top four categories. Charles Jordan, CEO of the Conservation Fund, felt that "no one took the time to engage us in the conservation movement."[21] Alison

Austin of Audubon spoke of how the "information about all these beautiful spaces is not targeted to us."[22] Others reiterated the importance of media and how the lack of stories and images of African Americans constitute a "not reaching out" by environmental organizations. When you don't see yourself, the message is, "you're not invited."[23]

- Public responses: Many black professionals believed the previous sentiment to be true for much of the white American population. In 1994, Jack Goldsmith wrote an article entitled, "Designing for Diversity" for the National Parks Conservation Association's magazine. In the article, he discusses the lack of African American and Latino visitors to the parks, despite increases in both populations across the country. Goldsmith goes on to address the need to incorporate "all aspects of experience and history" in park programs and suggests that an increase in minority hires would also increase the number of African American and Latino visitors (20). In the weeks that followed after this article was published, a quick response from the public ensued. Four of those letters were published in the magazine. All four had the same tone. One stated that the NPS should not spend time worrying about increasing diverse visitorship since everyone decides "out of their own free will" where to recreate. Another agreed, stating, "The visitors who do frequent the parks are there by personal choice, not by some undefined social bias that has been built into the park system." But perhaps the most blatantly racist comments were written by someone from Florida: "To modify the NP system to lure ethnic minorities would be a disaster and one more facet of our country that would be changed to please a few, ignoring the desires of the many. Bringing more minorities into the park would probably raise the crime rate when the rangers are being forced to spend more of their time in law enforcement than ever before." At the end of his letter, he pleads, "Please don't modify our parks to destroy our oasis" ("Letters to the Editor" 1994, 6).

The response to these letters was overwhelming. One man wrote, "It isn't as though I really need reminding that, despite much effort and considerable progress, ours is still essentially a racist nation." Many African American readers were not surprised. There needs to be "a genuine recognition by mainstream society that all Americans are equally valuable," states Audrey Peterman.[24] In an article Peterman wrote for the NPCA magazine (Autumn 2005), she elaborated on this point, writing about her love of the national parks and her belief that African Americans possess certain negative attitudes about the parks because of a history of racism in the United States. A letter to the editor chastised Peterman for putting a "racial spin" on her park experience and said it was a pity that black people need to "refer to themselves as hyphenated Americans" (*NPCA Magazine*, Winter 2006). David Herzberg Fenton goes on to say in his letter, "Mrs. Peterman states that 'issues of race, class, and privilege still continue to determine who belongs in the Great Outdoors.' She goes on to say 'attracting diverse visitors and employees remains an elusive goal.' How outrageous!" Much like the earlier letter-writers, Herzberg Fenton believes that desire is the sole determinant of whether or not African Americans engage with national parks. He does not consider that he is responding from a place of cultural privilege (as a white man). Furthermore, desire is shaped by how you imagine the world and consequently what you imagine is possible for you in the world. This "desire" is further fueled by what is reflected through media, policies, and institutions. Desire is considered by some to be a luxury determined by your life circumstances and how you feel you must prioritize your life. It is further informed by the information you have. If you lack awareness, how do make informed choices?

The worldview expressed by the individuals who wrote in defense of keeping the parks as they are is not an isolated case. Like many conservative voices across the social and political spectrum, they advocate for an agency they believe is the same for everyone, grounded in the "American master narrative" that refuses to consider the structural racism embedded in our way of life (Marable 2006). Conservative scholar Shelby Steele would no doubt agree with their assessment. During Steele's interview on C-Span, a caller shared a personal story of a young, smart black man who worked in an investment company and his inability to sign new investors because of the color of his skin. Steele responded by saying that he just needed to keep at it and be determined (he also stated that he "knew how this sounded"). By implication, the entire responsibility of the outcome was placed on the shoulders of the black man. Perhaps if he continued to knock on doors, a few might open (he went back to the Marine Corps instead). Shelby's advice does not address the structural reality that exists, nor does it offer effective strategies for dealing with the disillusionment that follows continual rejection.

For many of the black environmental professionals with whom I've spoken, these beliefs and attitudes feed into African American's lack of engagement and even outright fear of the environment. Gerrard Jolley, who at the time of our meeting worked at the National Park Foundation, reminded me that parks take on the characteristics of the place in which they are embedded. No one has ever said to African Americans in contemporary times, "it's OK now, you can come to the park."[25] Shelton Johnson, the black park ranger at Yosemite, recalled when someone called him "nigger" in a park setting. Many African Americans who work with community members felt that many of their constituents were afraid of two things: the unknown (primarily wildlife) and white people. While both wildlife and white people provoke fear in some constituents, the basis for, and the subsequent responses to, these fears are decidedly different. Wildlife is largely an unknown—many urban-dwelling African Americans have never had any real contact with wild animals outside of the zoo or dealing with raccoons or rabbits. Anything they have learned about wildlife they acquired from mass media or books. When visiting an area touted to have "wildlife," people tend to rely on those more knowledgeable (like park rangers) to guide them through the experience. On the other hand, most African Americans have had lifelong contact with white people. Fears about such contact are based on something that has happened to them, their family, their friends, or someone in their neighborhood. In addition, living with the knowledge of slavery, lynching, and racial profiling has meant that African Americans have had to develop survival skills in order to confront potentially life-threatening situations. They do not need to turn to an expert in order to deal with any given situation; they *are* the experts. While trust is needed to convince someone that they will be protected and secure while experiencing the outdoors, it is arguably more difficult to gain that trust in relation to fears held about white people than it is concerning fears about wild animals (more on the issue of fear in Chapter 6).

Sometimes blacks only intimated their concern about white people. They wouldn't say "white people" per se, but they would talk about feeling "alone" or being excluded or unwanted or refer to the "two-legged animal." Innuendos were followed by knowing looks and nods of heads. "If we're not afraid, we're crazy," said one interviewee.[26] "Being a black person, we know what we need to be afraid of," said another.

There is another element, which I call a "fatigue" that some African Americans expressed, which is reflected in their resistance to address their agency in confronting these barriers. Many are simply tired of being "the only one" at a largely white environment conference, meeting, or workshop and having to "explain" race and the environmental issues concerning the black community. After the Heart and Mind Environmental Leadership Workshop at the Garrison Institute, I had the opportunity to meet one of the African Americans who was invited, but didn't attend. When I asked her why, she explained that she was afraid of being the sole black voice, and the thought of that was just too exhausting. One of the African Americans I interviewed was blunt. She was "tired of talking to white folks about her experience" and had I been white, she would not have agreed to do the interview for this research.

For many African American professionals, particularly those who work in the NPS, the major challenge is dealing with the "old boys network" where diversity is seen as an expression of political correctness or as a goal that must occur within certain financial and time constraints. One NPS employee spoke about how some folks wanted Robert Stanton, the first African American to head the National Park Service, to resign because they got "tired" of dealing with these issues. Another NPS employee spoke about many "superficial things" that were done in the name of diversity and complained that things do not happen quickly. Besides, "when NPS superintendents are told to diversify their workforce, they don't always like being told anything."[27] For others, diversity is integral to any organization remaining relevant. Alan Spears of the NPCA described the impetus of his organization to promote diversity initiatives as "a straight recognition of the fact that the organization was not going to be relevant and politically effective if we didn't diversify our programs, programmatic outreach, staff, and membership."[28]

Some African Americans who acquire positions in mainstream environmental organizations face mistrust. "The predicament of outsiders who become insiders is a complex and longstanding problem" (Gainer and Torres 2002, 121). For these black individuals who appear to be straddling two different organizational worlds, the mistrust is generated among the grassroots who become concerned that their needs will not be prioritized as the "gatekeeper" struggles to maintain a double-consciousness within the larger institutional world. In order for the black gatekeeper to remain relevant in both worlds, that person must become adept in understanding, translating, and participating in ways appropriate to both communities. While the effort to do so is laudable, the "efforts of newcomers to think and act independently are slowly constrained by increasingly limited choices and the pressure exerted by those most invested in their producing certain outcomes" (Guinier and Torres 2002, 121).

Although conservation and protection of our environment is the most fundamental issue linking Americans and all humans, the all-white group on the cover of 2006 "Earth Day Issue" of *Vanity Fair* magazine dramatically illustrates the schism in America's thinking about the environment: Environmental protection is the forte of white people. "Environmental justice," which addresses the ill effects of pollution overwhelmingly experienced by the poor, is the forte of people of color. Never the twain shall meet, and there is little room for any other model. The problem with that is, everybody loses.
—Audrey Peterman, Earthwise Productions

One of the biggest challenges for individuals whose work is considered "environmental" is how quickly anything related to African Americans and the environment gets designated as an "environmental justice" concern. There is usually no discussion about the particulars—just the mere fact that "race" or "black people" are involved usually relegates African American environmental interactions to a particular point on the environment spectrum— environmental justice. Of course, there is nothing wrong with environmental justice. In fact, the field of environmental justice has done a stellar job at highlighting the complexity in framing any EJ discussion by drawing attention to three key debates within the EJ literature: whether environmental injustice is caused primarily by racism or capitalism; the value and importance of layperson knowledge vs. "expert knowledge"; and "the different ways to make the particular legible in reference to the abstract and the abstract accessible with reference to the particular" (Kurtz 2010, 102). However, my concern is with the assumption that the best framework to understand *any* environmental issue or experience had by African Americans is an environmental justice framework. Is EJ the best way to frame the black environmental experience? Is it the *only* way? What are some of the limitations of always using an EJ framework? Are we "shrinking our ledge"? What kinds of questions are we *not* asking as a result of always using EJ? How is African American participation in a broad array of environmental debates and events *assisted and constrained* by the use of EJ? How might we use triangulation to get at the multiple and complex issues concerning African Americans and the environment?

One well-known African American woman who has been consistently acknowledged for the environmental work she has done in a predominately African American and Latino community, related an incident that caused her consternation. She had been invited to an event along with Al Gore, to speak about her work. Standing backstage with the former vice president, she recognized the opportunity to engage him in a conversation about climate change. She was concerned that communities of color were not being actively engaged in the larger conversation, and she felt she had something to contribute. As she walked up to Gore, her nametag and organizational affiliation in clear view, she began what she hoped was a potentially fruitful dialogue. Instead, she was somewhat surprised when Gore slowly backed away while mentioning something about contributing money to EJ. When sharing with me this exchange, she was emphatic that she had no intention to ask him for money. Actually, she wasn't *asking* him for anything—she wanted to offer some ideas and thoughts on how to better engage a more diverse constituency in the climate change debate. Without speaking to Al Gore, we can never be quite sure of the motivation for his response. But how much of his response may have been influenced by the assumption that (1) this black woman is doing primarily EJ work, and (2) those doing EJ work are usually short on resources; and therefore, as a result, (3) she couldn't possibly have anything to *contribute*.

At the organizational level, there are also challenges. For more than twenty years, mainstream environmental organizations and self-identified EJ groups have waged an ideological and practical tug-of-war over what environmental issues should be prioritized and who should be involved in decision making concerning outcomes and applications. Less explicit, but playing a fundamental role in defining the tension between these two groups, is the way in which environmental terms, frameworks, and assumptions have been determined and implemented without consideration of how these "filters" can mute, mask, and erase the meanings inherent in a dialogue between two seemingly different entities. What can result are feelings of frustration, anger, and fatigue for EJ and other grassroots environmental groups, and a sense of misunderstanding, followed by a business-as-usual attitude for mainstream environmental organizations. For all concerned, the ability to think more expansively about their positions and their role in a changing environmental and social context is compromised.

These examples challenge the impulse to automatically consign any African American environmental experience to the field of environmental justice without considering (1) the basic assumptions one is making and (2) the potential consequences of perpetuating the idea that skin color is the primary determinant in one's ability to act and engage *all* environmental issues creatively and proactively.

To some degree, we are all complicit in "walking this talk," but what it denies is the possibility of a broader understanding of who African Americans are collectively and individually in relation to the environment. In addition, our ability to recognize a potentially game-changing contribution to an environmental challenge is compromised. The African American environmental relationship, like any human/environment relationship, is complex and always changing. Engaging the diversity of ideas within the black community on their own merit without automatically allocating them to a particular framework simply because of race creates the possibility of new collaborations and new iterations of human/environment interactions.

STRATEGIES: *Politics of Recognition*

For many professionals black or white, who work within an environmental organization or institution, it is important to generate dialogue across differences in order to create effective strategies. Specifically, there are four groups that have ongoing workshops and retreats that bring together diverse experiences and perspectives in hopes of developing new methods to combat old notions of race and difference.[29]

1. Summit 2005: Diverse Partners for Environmental Progress. Summit 2005, the national environmental summit, held in Wakefield, Virginia, established itself as a way to create space for ongoing conversation about environmental management by "building a strong network of advocates reflective of race, ethnicity, culture, class, and geography" ("Steps for the Future" 2005). For this ethnically and racially diverse group, the planners of the summit hired facilitators to ensure that all voices would be heard during the three-day workshop. When it came time to address the issue of racism, participants dealt with it directly through small-group work that was less intimidating than speaking one's mind in front of a large group. In this way, the groups had little problem with developing consensus that racism exists, and no problem articulating it and expressing frustration.

2. Garrison Institute. The Heart and Mind Leadership Project, sponsored by the Garrison Institute in New York State, had at its core the desire to develop environmental leaders "who are grounded in values, driven by vision and inspired by the sanctity of life" (draft document). As part of the three-day workshop, the conveners spoke about building a more inclusive and expansive movement. This group was all white; I was the sole exception. Discussion ensued about taking back "patriotism" and claiming a core set of values that most people share. Participants were concerned with figuring out how to tap into different social and faith-based movements in order to build a strong constituency. But some challenged that patriotism implies that one feels intrinsically part of a national identity and history that represents and supports you. To address this and other issues, "breakout sessions" were democratically chosen where participants could "go where they wanted" to carry on dialogue. However, on the issue of racism and diversity, these sessions proved to be more of a Band-Aid solution. Instead of dealing with what was right in front of them—the fact that there were no people of color in decision-making positions within the steering committee or at this workshop except for me—they chose to talk around the issue. While we all experienced some enlightenment at the end, crucial time that could have been spent creating real strategies was instead taken up by theoretical and anecdotal discussions.[30]

3. *The Center for Whole Communities (CWC).* Based in Waitsfield, Vermont, the center has developed forums and workshops where, according to their website, "diverse people and organizations can engage in honest dialogue about successes, failures, and highest aspirations" concerning people, land, and community. During the summer, they run three to four six-day retreats, which are fully funded for all participants, and they have Vision and Value workshops that they take to communities in order to engage leaders and community members in transformation and organizational change.[31] Participants in the summer retreats are "nominated" by previous attendees and include a wide range of professionals working in environmental organizations. Each retreat has twenty participants who meet on a farm run by founders Peter Forbes, who worked for the Trust for Public Lands for eighteen years, and his wife Helen Whybrow, working with Ginny McGinn, the executive director.

While a primary intention of CWC is to engender racial and ethnic diversity in their workshops and address racism in relation to land issues, they admittedly struggle with achieving their goals. Unlike the workshop at the Garrison Institute, Whole communities actively address their "shortcomings" and begin their assessments from that place. They have created a tool called "Measures of Health" to measure equity issues and "initiate organizational change, with the goal of being more open to the claims of others, collaborating authentically with new constituents, and honoring the larger meaning of the organization's work"("Measures" 2005). In addition, they conducted interviews with the people of color who attended retreats (myself included) as well as those who were invited but did not attend in order to understand how race shapes the attitudes, perceptions, concerns, and experiences of someone engaging in conversation with a largely white environmental movement. In addition, they've drafted a document called: *On Land, Race, Power, and Privilege: Our Draft Statement on Becoming an Anti-Racist Organization*, which addresses their role as a largely white organization in creating social change that strives to build healthy relationships between people and the land. They list the following as ways in which they are moving forward:

- Our staff and board are examining how racism and privilege operate within our organization's walls, coming to a deeper understanding of how they frame our decisions and determine the culture of our organization and learning how to change that culture.
- We are striving to diversify the leadership of our programs and the audiences they serve. We are meeting our goals of having at least one faculty member and at least 30 percent of the participants of our retreats be people of color.
- We offer full fellowships to our programs to remove financial barriers for participation, and we make available our facilities to groups working specifically on issues of race, power and privilege.
- We actively seek alliances with any organization working to overcome present injustices in the structure of land use and land access in this country.
- In all of our programs, we are committed to raise awareness about issues of oppression, power and privilege and to galvanize change around those issues within the environmental movement (http://www.wholecommunities.org/).
- By asking hard questions of themselves and not always relying on someone black to provide them with all the answers, the Center for Whole Communities allows for strategizing for change within their organization and in the larger environmental movement.[32]

4. Breaking the Color Barrier in the Great American Outdoors. Founded by Audrey Peterman in 2009, this conference, held in Atlanta, Georgia in September 2009, was the first in what was intended to be a biennial event. The primary purpose was to bring together an ethnically and racially diverse group of individuals and organizations from across the environmental spectrum to creatively address the challenges to engaging an increasingly culturally diverse American population in outdoor recreation and environmental management. In particular, emphasis was placed on building relationships between grassroots groups and national environmental leaders and generating support for youth participation in a broader environmental movement. One of the characteristics of this group that differentiates it from others mentioned above is the group's embracement of an expansive definition of environmental interaction. Participants included representatives from federal organizations such as Fish and Wildlife and the NPS, community and grassroots groups such as Sustainable South Bronx and Operation Green Leaves in Florida, and individuals like Captain Bill Pinkney, the first African American to sail around the world. Such a diverse group of individuals allowed for an increase in awareness about who is doing environmental work and the possibility of new iterations of working relationships to challenge old problems. While this conference was successful at creating new and building on existing relationships between various parties, there has not been a second gathering due to the challenge of attracting resources/funding, something experienced by many grassroots efforts.

SHIFTING THE GROUND

In his recent book on Hurricane Katrina, Michael Eric Dyson writes that "it is the exposure of the extremes, not their existence, that stumps our national sense of decency" (Dyson 2006, 3). While Dyson was talking about the lack of governmental response to victims of Katrina, the same could be said of those in the mainstream environmental movement concerning racism. When overt racism is apparent, these same people respond with appropriate rage and concern. But the day-to-day events that render black voices and concerns invisible and that perpetuate that invisibility/marginalization through stereotypical (mis)representations goes largely unnoticed.[33] To acknowledge that, as Dyson says about Katrina, "is to own up to our role in the misery of the poor" (Dyson 2006, 3). For some decision-makers in the environmental world, owning up to their role in maintaining structural racism is not something they want to embrace. This refusal or denial comes at a high price. "Denial of responsibility for racism permits the racial chasm to grow wider with each passing year" (Marable 2006, 21).

In this chapter, I have examined the ways in which racism, perceived or "real," can hinder the possibility of building long-term relationships of reciprocity between mainstream environmental groups and African Americans. In particular, the lack of consensus between African American environmental professionals and their white counterparts on whether or not racism and other exclusionary practices exist creates barriers to greater understanding and developing strategies designed to increase African American participation in environmental decision making.

Largely white environmental institutions and organizations that are interested in engaging African American communities need to prioritize working within their own four walls against racism first. In addition, these organizations must develop a healthy sense of respect for the culture, identity, leadership, and agendas of African American communities (Daniels 2002).

Furthermore, a renewed respect for American's collective history and in particular, an "authentic history of black people" that places African Americans at the center of a narrative will more accurately reveal the roots of the racialized landscape on which all Americans live (Marable 2006). When Americans deny the possibility of how this history has influenced our experiences, or when anyone frames the "race" discussion narrowly, all of us lose the opportunity to move forward in a more aggressive manner. To this end, "We [Americans] must reconstruct America's memory about itself, and our collective past, in order to re-imagine its future" (Marable 2006, 29).

Without engaging race, environmental practitioners run the risk of making environmental decisions with blinders on or through rose-colored glasses. How do environmental organizations and communities fashion new narratives that are inclusive and reflective of our past *and* offer new possibilities by expressing and acknowledging the complexity of our stories and the meanings we attach to them? A narrative that embraces our complex history can also provide us with greater insight into who we are, as Americans, and how we relate to each other. Narratives give people an opportunity to learn about power and the myriad ways in which it can be expressed. And a narrative that is rich in diverse detail has the power to provide us with tools to create a future that defies a limited imagination.

In a newscast marking the eve of the first anniversary of Hurricane Katrina's landing on the Gulf Coast, Brian Williams, the anchor of NBC Nightly News spoke about the need to address collectively the issues of "race, class, petroleum, and environment" (August 28, 2006). While America's relationship with petroleum has been part of a national conversation for some time, hearing a popular news anchor challenge Americans to engage in a similar discussion about race, class, and environment was both timely and radical. Williams is not only suggesting that a tangible relationship exists among race, class, and environment that can mean the difference between life and death (as so illustrated by Hurricane Katrina), but he is asking us to look beyond the devastating effects of Katrina to consider *how* this relationship is constructed and what American citizens might do to change that relationship for the better.

While discussions about race and environment within an academic context can prove valuable for understanding phenomena and in discovering methods to address the problems, scholars and researchers are continually challenged to connect their research with the present-day issues that all people encounter. In a way, Hurricane Katrina has given academics permission to have this conversation about race and the environment out loud, to bring theories and thoughts to bear that can translate into practical solutions and deeper understanding of the human condition. By linking academic research on race and environment to contemporary events like Katrina, scholars can continue to highlight the necessity to explore a complicated and emotional issue such as race, with honesty, respect, and rigor.

What if environmentalists changed the nature of the environmental debate to reflect emphasis on relationships instead of ownership in order to understand green spaces—land—and its "formative forces" both social and physical (Simpson 2002, 8)? In particular, environmental practitioners would pay closer attention to how social, political, and economic forces shape human relationships to the environment and to each other. In the United States, where race is woven into the fabric of our national identity, a profound understanding of those relationships requires the willingness of environmental institutions, organizations, and media to throw off the cloak of denial that keeps the "darkest aspects of Americas' past . . . hidden from plain view" ignoring how the past has the power "to shape the realities of our daily lives" (Marable 2006, 3). Whether we deny, accept, disbelieve, or forget these stories of the past, we are always working with a history that exists and informs our consciousness, ultimately finding its literal expression in the racialization and representations of the environment within institutions and the popular media.

CHAPTER SIX

The Sanctified Church

How Sweet It Is

We were good Americans, we were good citizens.
We loved our country, even if it didn't always love us back.

—Ruby Dee as Bessie Delaney in the film *Having Our Say:*
The Delaney Sisters' First 100 Years (1999)

Let's make a scarecrow!
But after we made it,
our field grew smaller.

—Richard Wright, #543

Let there be light!

—Zora Neale Hurston, from
I Love Myself When I Am Laughing

F
ear. In the Merriam-Webster dictionary, it is defined as: to have fear in; to have a reverential awe of; and, to be afraid of—some one, some place, some thing that is not necessarily easily defined or seen. In my capacity as a scholar-activist, and as an African American, I have been asked, particularly by white environmentalists, journalists, and scholars, about the role that fear plays in shaping the collective African American environmental relationship. Throughout this book, I have shared a few examples of how fear might inform that relationship, particularly in shaping the individual's perspective. In this chapter, I want to take a closer look at the roots of that fear and how we might shift our focus from the fear itself and instead, consider agency, motivation, and creativity as more deserving of our attention because of the potential for regeneration that these processes reveal.

In her book *Post Traumatic Slave Syndrome*, Dr. Joy DeGruy Leary sums up the question of fear this way:

One-hundred and eighty years of the Middle Passage, 246 years of slavery, rape and abuse; one hundred years of illusory freedom. Black codes, convict leasing, Jim Crow, all codified by our national institutions. Lynching, medical experimentation, redlining, disenfranchisement, grossly unequal treatment in almost every aspect of our society, brutality at that hands of those charged with protecting and serving. Being undesirable strangers in the only land we know. During the 385 years since the first of our ancestors were brought here against their will, we have barely had time to catch our collective breath. That we are here at all can be seen as a testament to our will power, spiritual strength and resilience. (DeGruy Leary 2005, 111–12).

For many of the African Americans that I have interviewed and spoken with, concern about one's safety from physical and or psychological harm was ever present in their environmental imaginary, regardless of where in the country they found themselves. Fear and mistrust of forests and other green spaces revealed a fear and mistrust of what these spaces represent in the eyes of a black person hobbled by repressive rules, cultural norms, racist propaganda, and the possibility of death. When we consider landscapes like national parks, or other areas of "natural" beauty, what you see is not always what you get. These places are overlaid with histories seen and unseen; geographies of fear that can make a "natural" place in the United States suspect to an African American. The experience is further enhanced by other aspects of difference, including gender, age, sexual orientation, geography, and experience. But when we take a bird's-eye view in trying to understand where fear manifests in the African American environmental relationship, we get glimpses into the complexities and into the cognitive dissonance experienced by black people and expressed through systems of oppression and individual circumstances/experiences.

And like any relationship, the one between African Americans and the natural environment is fluid, ever-changing, and informed by historical particularities and individual circumstances and predilections. Yet in all my conversations with African Americans, there appears to be an awareness of a larger cultural consciousness in the United States that either sidesteps, tiptoes around, or pushes back on race when considering the social, economic, and political boundaries (real and imagined) that shape the American way of life. Whether drawing on ancestral memory, historical "fact," or simply "driving while black" in today's world, this knowledge forms an integral part of black people's inner GPS and how they navigate white spaces.[1]

In the early 1990s, African American writer Evelyn C. White had been invited to teach creative writing in a summer workshop on the McKenzie River in Oregon, at the foot of the Cascade Mountains. The workshop participants were surrounded by hiking trails, lava beds, hot springs, and all manner of boat-trip possibilities on the river. But for White, there was something else lurking beneath the sweet sounds of summer emanating from her surroundings. "I wanted to sit outside and listen to the roar of the ocean, but I was afraid. I wanted to walk through the redwoods, but I was afraid. I wanted to glide in a kayak and feel the cool water splash on my face, but I was afraid. For me, the fear is like a heartbeat, always present, while at the same time intangible, elusive, and difficult to define. So pervasive, so much a part of me, that I hardly knew it was there" (White 1996, 283). The fear she experienced was largely informed by a collective history of violence against African Americans at the hands of white people. White recounts the story of Emmett Till and four little black girls who died in the bombing of the Sixteenth Street Baptist Church in Alabama. Even though these experiences are in the past, the residue of their meaning shaped her interactions in the present. It was not just fear of the unknown but also of what she knew about the "way it is" in the world to be a black woman/person. As in the above poem by Richard Wright, Evelyn put up "scarecrows" that she hoped would keep her safe. But they also limited the possibility of greater self-discovery and understanding.

Evelyn C. White is not alone in her concerns when considering a walk in the woods or a hike on a mountain. African American writer Eddy Harris believes that one of the primary issues for black people is "being vulnerable as a black person."[2] Bill Gwaltney's father is a bit more blunt: "There's a lot of trees in those woods and rope is cheap."[3] Dr. Joy DeGruy Leary would label these reactions "trans-generational adaptations associated with the past traumas of slavery and ongoing oppression," or Post Traumatic Slave Syndrome (PTSS). Living through a lifetime of slights, big and small, real and perceived, African Americans recognize, register, and adapt to a history of oppression often interpreted as a way to limit our existence. Whether in an office or a park, "We witness clear, unambiguous changes of behavior or language by whites toward us in public or private situations, and we code or interpret such changes as 'racial.' These minor actions reflect a structure of power, privilege and violence which most blacks can never forget" (Marable 2011, 8). Forests, parks and other areas of great natural beauty are

Figure 4. The "white" tree in the courtyard of Jena High School in Louisiana.
Photograph by Alan Bean.

not exempt from the psychological ramifications of an American history
steeped in oppressive tactics designed to diminish the humanity of one
group of people because of the color of their skin.

In Carolyn Merchant's book *Ecological Revolutions*, she discusses the
ways in which symbols shape "moods and motivations" within individuals, determining how they interact with nature and other human beings
(1989, 73). In the song "Strange Fruit," made famous by Billie Holiday and
Nina Simone, the southern tree becomes a symbol for the violence done
to black bodies, manifest as "strange fruit hanging from the poplar trees."[4]
The significance of this symbol—the tree as a harbinger of death for black
people—persists in contemporary culture whether in song, imagery, or as
part of the news of the day (Figure 4).[5]

But as with any icon, the meanings associated with the tree are
multiple and fluid, reflecting historical, geographical, and individual
idiosyncrasies.

For those black people living in the South during the twentieth century, the
tree also symbolized both economic opportunity and oppressive working

conditions for African Americans. Turpentine camps were rife throughout the South in the early and mid-twentieth century (the last camp in Georgia was closed in 2001). The camps were responsible for providing the pine-derived resources such as tar, turpentine, and pitch used for shipbuilding and repair. After cotton and tobacco, turpentine ranked as one of the South's major exports. And African Americans made up the majority of those working in this industry before and after the Civil War. The industry was so associated with African Americans, often referred to as "turpentine Negroes," that one turpentine operator went so far as to identity the quality of rosin (one of the products), by the shade of skin color of his workers and their families: a lighter color was of superior quality, while darker colored rosin got lower prices (Johnson and McDaniel 2006).

"The wilderness is benign; however, in the case of turpentine workers, it provided the backdrop or context for oppression" (Johnson and McDaniel 2006, 56). Turpentining occurred in remote pine forests, and the extraction of gum took place from March to November. Workers used tools to debark trees and chip them to get the gum flowing. The "chippers" might work five thousand trees a week, collecting the gum as it flowed into containers. In later years, chippers applied acid to make the gum flow more easily. Turpentining was brutal, dangerous, and back-breaking work. In addition, as a labor-intensive, extractive industry, it depended on cheap labor. Repressive contracts and labor laws broadly defined "vagrancy," making it practically illegal for males over the age of eighteen to be hanging out on the street corner. If "found" loitering, an African American man could be shipped to a turpentine camp and forced into labor (Johnson and McDaniel 2006).

Workers and their families lived in camps established by white operators that were essentially like plantations, in that the camps provided everything for the family: food, housing, and medicine. Many camps were considered hard, brutal, and isolated places with little social, educational, religious or recreational outlets. There were no unions, and workers had no rights. Bosses set the rules and could punish accordingly, often whipping workers to "instill fear and obedience" (Johnson and McDaniel 2006, 56). Some workers were even locked in their quarters so they couldn't leave. These practices were condoned by local authorities, who considered it appropriate to let white landlords/bosses handle African American misbehavior in any way they thought appropriate, which correlated with the views of the white majority (Johnson and McDaniel 2006).

While Frederick Jackson Turner argued that "wilderness promoted democracy, while civilized society, by contrast, fertilized tyranny because the very process of civilization compelled one to conform," the experience of turpentine workers reveals "the worst kind of despotism" and not the "rugged individualism" espoused by white environmental proponents in regard to having a wilderness experience (Johnson and McDaniel 2006, 56).

SPACE, THE FINAL FRONTIER?

Space was circumscribed for enslaved Africans and black laborers while on a white owner's property (plantation, farm, or camp), but was it possible to attain a different sense of space in some wild areas unsullied by a white presence? Cheryl Harris, in her piece on *Whiteness as Property* explains that it is not race alone that oppressed African Americans and American Indians, but the interaction of race and property that maintained "racial and economic subordination" (1993, 277). When finding themselves in a space where whiteness as a presence either in metaphorical or literal terms was not apparent, were black people unencumbered by the strictures of race and their own fears? As a "space of possibility," the Great Dismal Swamp provides insight into how enslaved Africans shaped "the North American landscape"—in particular, how they "expressed their autonomy, restored their dignity, and even achieved their freedom . . . through the manipulation of the very landscapes designed to restrict them" (Ellis and Ginsburg 2010, 3). The experience of black people in the Great Dismal Swamp reveals how runaway slaves navigated what DeGruy Leary calls the "cognitive dissonance" of American life—where the presupposition that "all men are created equal" is in tension with the reality of slavery, land dispossession, and the "natural" ebb and flow of the swamp itself. How did they navigate the swamp, slavery, and their own fears? Can we draw a parallel between the abandoned lots of today (think Detroit) and how black communities reclaim these spaces, and the black experience of the swamp?

The Great Dismal Swamp (GDS) National Wildlife Refuge covers a vast expanse of approximately 112,000 acres of forested wetlands, with the largest natural lake in Virginia, Lake Drummond, at its center. According to the website, people have lived and worked in the GDS for approximately thirteen thousand years. Specifically, African and African American "maroons" (runaway slaves) fleeing from plantations would find refuge within the swamp. Between 1720 and 1860, thousands of maroons lived there "on high ground in cabins or shacks, grew their own food and hunted, and augmented their supplies through pilfering at farmsteads peripheral to the swamp" (Sayers 2005, 12). Maroons built a life for themselves; according to archeologist Daniel O. Sayers, documents reveal that they even had "their own system of governance, had strict rules in order to maintain safety," and in some cases, they were raising children who had never seen the face of a white person (13). Here I must offer a caveat: one must be careful to not romanticize the experience of maroons living in the GDS. The terrain was hazardous and, at times, impenetrable. Black people building a life in the swamp were also living under the continuous fear of being discovered. Slave owners did not relinquish their hold on their human property that easily. "One of the most widespread methods of tracking runaways was to use highly trained so-called 'negro dogs'" (Franklin and Schweninger 1999, 160). Disgruntled slave owners organized "drives," inviting hunters to bring their dogs who were specifically trained to track down people hiding out in the swamp. Between the challenges of negotiating the swamp itself and avoiding recapture by slave owners, the life of a maroon in the GDS consisted of "habitual caution and watchfulness" (Simpson 1990, 76).

Yet despite the challenges of day-to-day living in the swamp, any fear of the swamp was tempered by a more enduring fear of the white population, slavery, and negative notions of blackness that were embedded in the dominant culture. The wilderness, as defined in contemporary terms, became a place of refuge and possibility for black people. Maroon sites, such as the African and African American enclaves in the GDS "can be read against the legal landscape and the geographies of power and resistance rather than as commonplace sites within the economic system of slavery" (Laroche 2010, 258). One might even go so far as to label parts of the GDS during this historical period as a "black landscape"—a "system of paths, places, and rhythms that a community of enslaved people created as an alternative, often as a refuge, to the landscape systems of planters and other whites" (Ginsburg 2010, 54). An acknowledgment of a black landscape is also a recognition of another "way of looking at one's surroundings" and recalibrating one's movements and thoughts to create "a distinctive black geography" (56). Theorizing black experience on the landscape in this way is not to deny the larger systems of oppression that defined the economic, political, and cultural milieu. Instead, we are offered an opportunity to expand how we view resistance and resilience in their multiple manifest forms on the landscape. And we are reminded that "beyond the eye and mind of the white majority, African American culture was vibrantly alive, and had been alive for more than three hundred years. Through that span, African Americans combined African legacy with American culture, and along the way they left stories in the ground" (Ferguson 1992, 123).

In Zora Neale Hurston's classic text, *The Sanctified Church*, writer Toni Cade Bambara describes African Americans as "a people who not only survived the 'peculiar institution' of the South, but have survived to 'make new' their own realities of community and tradition" (1981, 7). Here in the United States, there are "historical and contemporary spaces," (including slavery, Jim Crow segregation, economic disenfranchisement, racial profiling) in which African Americans have survived and thrived, revealing a "geographical intelligence" that defies ongoing attempts to bound black life through cultural mores and norms, policy, and law. Whether it was runaway slaves in the Great Dismal Swamp or black artists on the streets of Detroit, African Americans have revealed great skill at adapting to environments seen and unseen that challenge our very existence. Despite the interventions designed to restrict, subvert, and deny black life on the American landscape, African Americans utilize agency, identity, and civic engagement as a means to expand this narrative of disenfranchisement. Adaptiveness, resilience, fearlessness, and courage wasn't the anomaly, but was the reality. While fear as a by-product of white supremacy and oppression was/is certainly part of the lived reality for many African Americans, focusing solely on the fear denies the malleability of the black imagination to create and construct a rich reality that is not grounded primarily in fear, but in human ingenuity and the rhythms and flows of life. This reorientation of focus allows for the greater possibility of engaging black contributions to ecological challenges that may fall outside the confines of state-sanctioned environmental practices that are grounded in the dominant environmental narrative.

I read an article in the *New York Times* that used the phrase "poetic human" to describe all the ways in which we engage the world, particularly those ways that cannot be measured, "scientized," or standardized. "It is in the irritating human realm where the interesting difficulties are, and where one might have to really think about and deal with an individual's history, circumstances and reactions. It is the attempted standardization of a human being and of a notion of achievement that is limiting, prescriptive and bullying" (Kureishi 2012).

I often think of how my parents engaged with the world around them. For my parents' fortieth wedding anniversary, my father gave my mother a young cherry blossom tree. Planted on the hill, on that estate, we could see the tree grow day after day, outside the kitchen window. When my parents left their home, they could not take the tree with them because the roots of the tree were deeply embedded and the tree itself had unwittingly become a significant part of the landscape. When I think about the relationship between African Americans and the environment, I can't help but consider the myriad possibilities in our collective future that have roots in our complex and often painful past. "There is a reclaiming process that can take place," says Evelyn C. White.[6] Whenever I see a cherry blossom tree, I think of my parents and their commitment to a life that would support and grow their children. I am also reminded of the power to transform; how a tree can come to symbolize multiple meanings; and how the nature of a place/space and our relationship to that space can be reborn and reimagined.

HOW SWEET IT IS

Since the moment when I began doing this research in earnest in 2004, there has been a surge in creative movements, activities, and interventions within the black community (and elsewhere) that continues to seek ways to synthesize what we understand about life, our experiences, and the day-to-day processes that shape, inform, and transform our relationship to the environment. From the green economy to "bees in the hood," black people are redefining justice and environmental activism, challenging academics and policy makers to rethink and reframe environmental strategizing. While many seeds are being planted and taking root, guerilla greenies and people such as Van Jones, Brenda Palms Barber, Pearl Fryar, and Tyree Guyton have become the public faces promoting, explaining, and titillating our intellectual senses and our practical impulses to consider new ways of seeing and being green.

One of these explosions in creativity is the idea of the green economy. Van Jones, the founder for Green for All in Oakland, California, believes in a "clean energy future where everyone has a place—and a stake." In his book, *The Green Collar Economy: How One Solution Can Fix Our Two Biggest Problems*, Jones promotes the idea of eco-populism, challenging the green movement to "attract and include the majority of people, not just the majority of affluent people." He believes that this can be done by meeting people where they live, showing images of black and brown peoples engaged in creative and regenerative environmental activities, and speaking "to the economic and health opportunities that 'ecological' solutions can provide" (2008, 98). By figuring out what we're for instead of continually citing what we're against, Jones challenges us to reframe the larger environmental conversation and work collectively toward common goals.

Another powerful vision hails from the mean streets of Chicago, home to Oprah and the first black president. Brenda Palms Barber had an idea. In 1999, she moved from Denver to Chicago to become the executive director of the Northlawn Employment Network where she thought her primary focus would be to help build a consortium that focused on job readiness by addressing capacity challenges. She discovered that the community wanted a direct service agency—someone who could help them find jobs. So Palms Barber conducted a two-year assessment to understand the high unemployment rate and the community's needs. What she found was that approximately 57 percent were men and women who were ex-offenders; of that 57 percent, 80 percent were men who were previously incarcerated, and most of these men were African American. These men and women were suffering from skill shortages and the stigma of being previously incarcerated. Brenda focused on creating a job readiness program she called "U-turn Permitted" to address the needs of formally incarcerated men and women. "People can turn their lives around," says Palms Barber. And she set out to prove it. For a while, the program was quite successful—her organization saw anywhere from two hundred to three hundred people a month. But after 9/11 and the passing of the Patriot Act, potential employers, motivated by the fear of terrorism, began conducting background checks. Consequently, many of the formerly incarcerated lost their jobs. "I felt at that moment, I had to do something" to help create jobs for people, Palms Barber admitted. But aside from the challenge of finding employment for ex-offenders in a post-9/11 world, Brenda faced other roadblocks. She was an outsider, and Northlawndale, one of the most studied areas in the United States, had seen many people come and go in the quest to build their resumé experience. What was going to make Palms Barber different? She realized that in order to honor her commitment to the community, she was going to have to build a business that generated income to support the nonprofit. She needed to diversify her funding stream in order to be able to stay in Northlawndale for the long haul. "I personally felt an obligation."[7]

She contemplated a number of ideas: starting a temp agency, but that proved too risky; a landscaping company, but she didn't have a competitive advantage; a delivery service, catering to the many elderly residents in Northlawndale who couldn't get around, but bringing together ex-offenders and the elderly didn't sit well with everyone. One day, she was sharing with a friend her frustration in trying to come up with a good—no—a great job idea. Her friend mentioned that she knew someone who was a beekeeper and that you didn't need a degree because knowledge was passed down by word of mouth. Palms Barber found this idea quite attractive: no focus on academic achievement, and an oral tradition as the vehicle for sharing knowledge (and African American culture has a rich history of story telling). The idea of beekeeping started her creative impulses buzzing. She admits that when she first shared the idea with others, they would usually say things like, "What are you talking about? Are you crazy?" She didn't get much positive reinforcement at the beginning. But then she sat down with friend and visionary thinker Paula Wolff, who listened, paused, and said, "What a sweet beginning." "At that moment, says Palms Barber, "I knew I had the name." And so Sweet Beginnings was born.

Sweet Beginnings is in the business of working with previously incarcerated men and women to review and renew their strategies, skills, and interactions with other people, places, and processes around them. Palms Barber worked with beekeepers, corrections officers, and those knowledgeable about business to start Sweet Beginnings, a company that makes urban honey and honey-related products. In particular, she focused on getting educated about bees and local beekeepers, and many people volunteered their time, knowledge, and experience, and assisted Palms Barber in getting her vision off the ground. Like any new venture, Palms Barber was challenged on many fronts. While she viewed tension as a place of creative possibility, not everyone felt the same. Power, that is, who gets to claim and disseminate knowledge, and different perspectives on where the business should be headed, meant that some old relationships had to die to make room for new relationships so that the vision might grow. In 2007, Sweet Beginnings, supported by a new business plan, began making new and improved products and had an executive director who could tell you everything you ever wanted to know about bees. She has even helped design a certificate program at Wilbur Wright Community College where men and women from the community can take Beekeeping 101. For those men and women who worked for Sweet Beginnings, she was able to assist them in developing their skill set and build their self-esteem. And she got an added bonus—she became an accidental "greenie." Now she intentionally infuses green business principles in the work that she does: the product they produce is local, African Americans can reclaim their relationship to the earth through beekeeping, and she believes that "through green" people can become empowered. Sweet Beginnings products are sold at Whole Foods and other high-end stores in the Chicago area, and you can buy the products online. "People need to be reminded that they are important and can make a positive contribution," says Palms Barber.

Sweet Beginnings takes green to a whole new level. Not only does it challenge old models of engagement regarding "outreach" and "diversity," but "green" expands to include the experiences and the needs of the people that the business is purported to serve. In addition, Sweet Beginnings taps into the resources of the community, both people and the flora that had previously been ignored and abandoned. "People viewed as second-class people can make a first-class product," says Palms Barber. "People need to be reminded that they are important."

Tyree Guyton, an African American artist living in Detroit, would most likely agree. For the last twenty-five years, Guyton has been working at the intersection of art, abandoned outdoor spaces, and economically challenged communities of color to create new strategies for engaging environmental and economic change. "Taking the detritus, or discards, of life and allowing the elements to participate in the creative process is how I give life back to the canvas." And in Guyton's case, the "canvas" is often an abandoned lot or building, or an entire street that he reenvisions. The Heidelberg Project was born out of Guyton's need to address his community where "drugs, crimes, prostitution and gangs" defined the landscape. "I watched, in horror, the deterioration of my neighborhood," Guyton remembers.[8] By embracing what others have preferred to turn away from, Guyton has created another way for us to think about and frame conversations around race, class, and place. Whether it's an old tree that he fills with old shoes, or a house that he covers in polka dots and "junk," Guyton pushes us past our limitations and asks academics, policy makers, and strategists to consider the human/environment relationship anew. As one admirer states, "As icons of imaginative life [projects like the Heidelberg project] are emblems of resurrection, of the capacity of individuals—arguably, even of communities—to re-create themselves from ruins, with or without official involvement."[9]

In Bishopville, South Carolina, on Route 145, you will find the home of Pearl and Metra Fryar. Pearl, as he is known, is the son of a black sharecropper who has brought new life to an agricultural-based community through his topiary artistry that has garnered international attention. When he and his wife were in their sixties, they bought a home in predominately white Bishopville, an impoverished rural community. They heard that some people were less than enthusiastic about their impending arrival because of a belief that "black people don't keep their yards looking nice." Instead of simply feeling angry, Pearl saw this as an opportunity. With little to no horticultural skills, he decided to turn his three-and-a-half-acre yard into a work of living art. Using discarded plants from a nearby nursery, he would nurture them back to life. Once they were full grown, he would begin the process of reshaping trees and bushes in accordance with his vision. With ladders, lights, and electric saw in hand, he would work well into the night to create his masterpiece (which could take years), turning once discarded trees and plants into something that challenged the eye, as well as the ingrained perspectives of long-time white locals. "When he's in the garden, it's man relating to Nature," says his wife, Metra. Today, thousands of tourists come from all around the world to Bishopville to see Pearl's garden, contributing to the local economy and the buzz surrounding Pearl. Horticultural groups nationwide are eager to engage his expertise and energy. And perhaps what is most important, Pearl has single-handedly put a dent in old racial attitudes about black people and the outdoors (in this case, their yards). When Pearl was asked about how he does this, he just says, "I don't go by the book. And my book is gonna be what you don't find in the other books" (Fryar 2008).

CONCLUSION

There is an African American letterpress printer, Amos Kennedy Jr., who runs a company called Kennedy Prints! (originally based in Alabama, but moved to Detroit in 2013). Kennedy is known for "stirring up strong emotions and encouraging people to think in previously unexplored ways."[10] So I asked Kennedy if he could produce a poster about my book (Figure 5), as I was interested in seeing how he would engage the ideas I presented in these pages. He agreed and asked me to send him words: the book title, chapter titles, and anything else I would like to share with him. So I sent him book excerpts, along with titles he requested. He explained to me that he uses a layering process, sometimes employing as many as six layers to create the image that he believes represents the meaning behind the words. In doing so, he creates the possibility for the viewer to engage the piece in multiple ways, thereby producing diverse responses and possibilities of seeing differently. So, taking a cue from his process, I would like to briefly revisit some of the themes that I have explored in this book and ask the reader to think about each chapter as a layer meant to incite and provoke the emergence of ideas and praxis previously unconsidered. Finally, I would like to offer some of my own thoughts of where we might begin.

Throughout this book, I have explored a number of issues. Informed by empirical research, feminist and critical race theory, environmental history,

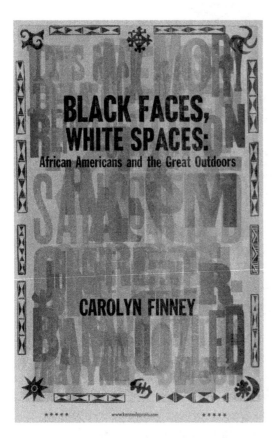

Figure 5. Poster by Amos Kennedy Jr. of Kennedy Prints!, commissioned by the author in 2012.

geographical thought, and cultural studies (in particular, art, music, and film), I set out to get a better understanding of the African American environmental relationship in the United States. In particular, by engaging black voices (including my own) from multiple cultural sites, I worked to bring into relief a tapestry of experience that reflects multiple strands of knowledge production, dissemination and expressions of presence on the landscape that reveal a relationship that is complex, sometimes contradictory and always ever-present.

In the preface and the introduction, I introduced a number of components that I felt were necessary in pursuing this exploration of the African American environmental relationship. In particular, I signify how the personal, for myself and many of the African Americans whose stories fill these pages, is intricately connected to a past history and a present experience, defining perceptions, beliefs, and impulses to action. As the researcher and writer of this study, my voice has also been influenced by an American history of race and environment that has informed the way I did the research and my approach to writing this book. My choice to direct this book to a diverse audience as opposed to simply those who study in my field is reflective of my understanding of how disciplinary silos can limit the emergence of intellectual and creative relationships and approaches. And while I take sole responsibility for how this book is written, many African Americans contributed to this narrative. As such, to include their experiences, ways of knowing, and observations it was necessary for me to access cultural spaces where African Americans have been able to produce and disseminate information about themselves *by* themselves.

In Chapter 1 I applied the second layer. Borrowing a theme from African American director Spike Lee, I explored how we have been bamboozled into accepting a narrative about the American relationship to land and the environment that has managed to subsume those parts of history we have (arguably) not fully reconciled (such as slavery and the forced removal of American Indians from their land). This flattening out of the American story is reflected in policy, cultural representations, and the tension between African Americans and the mainstream environmental movement. There is a flow of creative and intellectual energy between the cultural spaces we inhabit and the political and intellectual spaces that qualify, quantify, and legitimate our collective histories in specific ways. For African Americans, our involvement in anything environmental can be marginalized, reinterpreted, forgotten, misunderstood, or simply ignored.

The trajectory of the American environmental narrative also included a dalliance with the eugenics movement in an attempt by a privileged few to unite culture, natural resources, and national identity as central to the nation-building project. Chapter 2 adds complexity by exploring our conflicted relationship with race, nature, and nation where all men (and women) are not created equal. The American relationship to nature and race reveals a cognitive dissonance between principles associated with the creation of a United States and the actual cultural, political, and intellectual practices and permutations that decidedly tell a different story. Whether in the seemingly separate but equal growth/creation of the Wilderness Act and the Civil Rights Act in 1964, or in the use of primates in visual and textual representations meant to directly or indirectly imply blackness, the relationship between African Americans and the environment has revealed multiple sites (cultural, political, intellectual) that continue to expose how that relationship is perceived and depicted today.

With Chapter 3, I add a fourth layer that considers that memory isn't simply something that African Americans access for personal reasons. Collective and individual memory is seen as a source of legitimation of our experience and provides insight into who we are and how we see the larger world. We begin to see how slavery and the removal of four hundred thousand acres of land from black owners informs a contemporary relationship with the land and the environment. More important, the desire and the need to validate our presence and experience on American soil has inspired many African Americans to use memory as a source of legitimation and inspiration.

Visual and cultural representations can influence both popular perception and personal belief about one's self and one's relationship to the larger world. In Chapter 4, I delved more deeply into the power representational processes have to shape identity and inform how Americans perceive and relate to African Americans, particularly in an environmental context. Hurricane Katrina is one example of how framing and naming this environmental disaster revealed racialized perceptions of black people that perpetuate negative depictions and stereotypes that have consequences for organized efforts to engage African American communities. Embedded within these images and depictions are fundamental beliefs about who black people are and by inference who we can be.

In Chapter 5, I add another layer where I looked at African American participation in environmental activities in communities, organizations, and in their own lives. History, representations, memory, and narratives about who we are—all explored in the previous chapters/layers—gird, support, inform, guide, and disrupt how African Americans think about and actively engage in environmental work. But these histories and narratives also inform their white counterparts within environmental organizations and can hinder the ability of the organization to produce a joint commitment to and understanding of what it means to engage diversity. Furthermore, for African Americans doing environmental work, there is often a tension between the needs of the organization and the desire to serve the African American community. The personal and the professional become intertwined, and the African American environmental professional can be forced to make some difficult choices. What can result is a form of fatigue and frustration on all sides by those concerned with diversity, thereby limiting creative options and the chance to build stronger relationships.

With Chapter 6, I add the final layer that considers the sanctified nature of the black experience with the environment in the United States. On one hand, you have the ever-present fear on the part of African Americans in response to historical and present-day acts of oppression (such as slavery and racial profiling) that can stifle the human impulse to move forward. On the other hand, recognition of their ability to make a choice to survive and thrive despite these difficulties have inspired African Americans to produce creative responses to environmental and social challenges that point to the possibility of not only seeing differently, but doing differently.

Van Jones, Brenda Palms Barber, Pearl Fryar, and Tyree Guyton and the many others mentioned in this book give us hope. We can rebuild our human/environment relationships through examination of our existing relationships to each other, different communities, our social norms, narratives and beliefs, and the natural environment. Innovative thinkers and doers such as these practice a digging deep, a fearlessness, an expansion of the mind, a stretching of what they know so as to provide all of us with the opportunity to do the same.

What does this mean for practitioners, cultural instigators, geographers, critical race theorists, and others? While I would not be so bold as to offer a broad prescription to everyone, I do have some thoughts about where we each might begin. I am privileged to work with many exceptional environmental practitioners who are clearly committed to moving forward, but are often stuck on how to actually do this (particularly white practitioners). Their organizations need to see deliverables, and so many are forced to start "doing" without any real assessment made of the cultural competency of the organization (or themselves). Building relationships across difference means you have to do the internal work, both within the organization and within oneself, before you start reaching out to individuals and communities. How are you building relationships across difference within your organization and your own life? You know that saying, "wherever you go, there you are"? You carry with you your own limitations, biases and unawareness, and that of the organizations into any new relationship. It's not that you need to be perfect; but you need to know exactly where you're at in your own growth in order to meet someone else with honesty and clarity, and in order to do no harm.

For those who operate primarily in cultural spaces—producing images, writing stories, making art and music—continue to be bold and honest in your work. But also do the work of confronting your own biases and consider your intention *and* the impact your work will have on others. This is particularly true for those whose work is about race and difference. I read that those responsible for the *Vogue* cover shoot, after being shown the

1917 Mad Brute poster and the striking similarities it had with their cover, responded by saying that "they didn't know" or realize that their cover was so similar to the poster. While I am more than a little suspicious of this response (did I say the similarities were *striking*?), "I didn't know" just isn't good enough anymore, even if it is true. Are you ready to attend to the impacts your lack of knowing might have on a person or a community? What I found most disturbing about the *Vogue* cover was not the image itself, but the lack of willingness by those responsible to open up a conversation about their own limitations and biases and about race and the media. There was an opportunity for growth and relationship building that they all but ignored.

As an African American geographer, one of my biggest challenges within the discipline is engaging race in a way that doesn't "ghettoize" the work and doesn't fall into the trap of only recognizing/acknowledging ways of conceptualizing and understanding race that fit into the disciplinary canon. I believe this would be true for many academic disciplines that strive to provide strong empirical and theoretical work that inform and legitimate practice and policy out in the world. I also understand that the work of geographers in particular and academics in general is informed by a system of production and dissemination of knowledge that can unwittingly ignore, dismiss, or just overlook other types of knowledge production. While there are a number of excellent geographers who are actively doing cross-disciplinary work (many of whom I continue to learn from), I would like to see geography open up to engaging nonacademic spaces of knowledge production with the same respect given to more traditional spaces, such as academia. In particular, when doing work about race and difference, I find it is imperative to engage cultural work—be it popular culture, art, or music in all its myriad forms—because it is in these spaces that people who are "different" are able to produce work about themselves without the boundaries and rules that can inhibit their voices that more traditional ways of knowing are unable to accommodate.

My work continues to be influenced by critical race theory. In particular, those African American theorists who have committed their intellectual energies to exploring and explaining the black experience have long impacted my work and my life. What I would be excited to see is more work by these theorists that explicitly considers the nature of the African American environmental relationship. What has become clear to me in doing this research and writing this book is that African Americans have distinctive and powerful perspectives and ideas about the environment. What has also become clear is that we don't always play by someone else's rules, sometimes out of necessity, sometimes out of our sheer determination to be heard. I believe critical race theorists are in a prime position to influence the conversation on race and the environment, both for policy makers and environmental organizations, and for African Americans themselves.

Now I come to what is perhaps the group of people I am most passionate about. I have been privileged to know so many African Americans, from my family, to friends, colleagues, neighbors, and those I admire from a distance—who continue to think broadly, take risks, and pursue their environmental work with nothing short of imagination, commitment and love. What I would ask, for myself and others, is that we not only keep resisting oppression and the suppression of who we are, but we actually continue to expand and evolve how we come to know and who we might become.

Our resilience is a reflection of our need to survive, yes. I think Darwin was on to something. But our resilience becomes multidimensional and explosive with possibilities because of what we believe we can create. And creation does not exist in a vacuum. There is something about our collective experiences—the "collective" sometimes defined by cultural/ethnic/racial differences—and the relationship between those differences that offers a chance to recognize and embrace our common humanity; a chance to imagine other possibilities by seeing another's position of privilege and the challenges one has experienced. We come to understand how people create, retain hope, and move forward. Our mutual responsibility is to see those differences and recognize the possibilities and be fearless enough to bring those possibilities into our realities.

I could have told the collective story of any group of people, as I believe everyone's story is rich with possibility and revelation. I share with you this one story/interpretation of the African American environmental experience in order to illuminate the connections between what we do and think and who we believe we are; how actions and beliefs can be institutionalized and systematized ultimately to the detriment of us all. Systems and institutions only recognize "difference" on their own terms, which are static and limited. How do we move forward and support ideas and manifestations that do not fit the standard narrative or value system?

These stories are lessons in seeing—seeing who we are and who we can be. They are meant to guide us in our envisioning—vision-making for ourselves, for our communities, for our world. We have the power to bring those visions into material reality. Human beings have been doing it since the beginning of our existence, whether it was holding people in bondage or going to the moon. We have the chance to see differently, imagine differently, and be actively involved in the regeneration of our communities, in the broadest sense. When we know different, we do different. It is in this spirit that I continue to hear the voices and experiences of those who have shared with me their present visions for the future.

Epilogue

Would America be America without her Negro people?
—W. E. B. Du Bois, *The Souls of Black Folk*

Not long ago, I was visiting my parents in Leesburg, Virginia, and they told me about a letter they had received from one of their old neighbors in Mamaroneck, New York. Enclosed in the note from their neighbor was a letter from the Westchester Land Trust. The trust had determined that the property my family lived on and worked for fifty years had "extensive scenic, naturally wooded frontage" and because it's in the Mamaroneck River Watershed (the river is subject to flooding), protecting the property from further development could help prevent further flooding. The trust also determined that the large, permanent pond on the property is a significant habitat for fish, turtles, and waterfowl. In addition, there are also mallards, blue herons, wild turkeys, and deer. None of this was news to my parents, of course. But the trust wanted to inform the neighbors that the new owner of the estate had generously donated a conservation easement on the land to the Westchester Land Trust. Which means that the property which contains the new owner's home (and the house I grew up in), will never be further developed and the trust will ensure that its conservation values are protected. What caught my attention was how the author of the letter thanked the current owner for his "generosity and conservation-mindedness," but says nothing about my parents, who cared for that land for fifty years, with no "conservation easement" or other environmental incentives. I believe that my parents are part of a larger story of people seen and unseen whose relationship to the environment is one forged in sweat, ingenuity, necessity, and a little true grit. For those of us concerned with the relationship between humans and the environment in this time of great change (environmental, social, and economic), it behooves us to acknowledge and engage the unlikely and unfamiliar (be it people or ideas) in our attempt to grasp our future with clear intention and eyes wide open.

I went to an exhibit at the Corcoran Gallery of Art in Washington, D.C. It was entitled, "30 Americans." In fact, all thirty artists whose work was represented were African Americans. But they chose to collectively represent themselves as Americans first and foremost. "Each artist reckons with the notion of black identity in America, navigating such concerns as the struggle for civil rights, popular culture, and media imagery."[1] Their work—much of it infused by race and difference, was a reminder not only that they are black, but that they are participants in an on-going nation-building project of who we are as American peoples. The struggle, the joy, the sheer artistry of living manifest in their work was a reminder that our *collective* history in this country cannot be denied. Just like "nature," the legacy of human experience on this soil will always find a way to express itself.

I had the pleasure to meet a young, talented African American teenager named Aisha who had participated in a program sponsored by the NPS and Latino American Youth Type Center in Washington, D.C. This past summer, through a program focused on the arts, African American and Latino teenagers were taken out on camping trips to national parks in the D.C. area, many for the first time. Afterward, the young women and men were prodded to share what they had experienced through music and painting. Some participated in a mural project at the National Zoo. Some wrote powerful slam poetry about climate change. And others, such as Aisha, wrote songs about their relationship to the natural environment. Their visions of the world expressed through painting, spoken word, and song were painful, funny, hopeful, and real. While I can only speak for myself, I had a feeling that the other adults in the room were also inspired by the thoughtfulness and possibility inherent in what we heard. Vision belongs to us all—we just need to be able to recognize and support it. So I'd like to end this book with the words of fourteen-year-old Aisha, in all her youthful wisdom: "We have to keep thinking of tomorrow, today."

Notes

1. I do not mean to imply that African Americans no longer need to be strategic. In a recent *New York Times* article (December 5, 2009), African Americans admitted to "whitening" their resumes by downplaying or concealing African American affiliations, and in some cases even their names, in order to have a better chance of getting a good job.

2. In her article entitled, "The Personal Is Political, but Is It Academic?," Mary Patrice Erdmans explores the role of personal narrative in "scholarly" texts. In particular, she underscores how narrative methods reveal that all stories are constructed and that reflexivity helps to articulate power differences and reveals how "the narrative is influenced by the author's relation to the ethnic group" (2007, 9).

3. I had the privilege of hearing Dr. Bernice Johnson Reagan speak at the Black Environmental Thought II conference in September 2012. Among her many accomplishments as a social activist, scholar, and artist, Dr. Reagan was a distinguished professor of history at American University and was named curator emeritus at the Smithsonian Institute in 1994 where she had worked for nearly twenty years.

4. The apt remark is from writer and friend Valerie Boyd.

INTRODUCTION

1. For example, Kimberley Smith (2004), in her article entitled "Black Agrarianism and the Foundations of Black Environmental Thought," states that nineteenth-century black writers, by focusing on black farmers, "property rights, [and] the status of labor and the exploitation of workers," emphasized what was important to the black community concerning humans' relationship to the environment.

2. It is primarily mainstream environmental practitioners that perceive a lack of response by African Americans to environmental issues. A more recent study by Paul Mohai (2003) counters that belief by revealing results from the General Social Surveys that suggest that African Americans "are as likely as whites to take actions on behalf of the environment" (Mohai 2003, 21). African Americans are just finding alternate avenues to express their concerns, not necessarily through mainstream environmental organizations.

3. While a detailed consideration of gender is outside the parameters of this book, it is important to note that my choosing to focus on race is not to deny the significance of gender as an integral component to understanding African American identity and the African Americans' relationship to nature and outdoor spaces. My choice to limit

my analysis to race as a defining characteristic of the African American environmental relationship is a direct response to the empirical data I collected, which revealed that race, more than any other kind of "difference" was the aspect of identity that consistently presented common themes/connections regardless of gender, class, and geographical particularities. Having said that, there are a number of scholars who look at various permutations related to gender, race, blackness, and nature/environment including Donna Haraway, bell hooks, Laura Pulido, and Angela Davis.

4. Environmental justice advocates contend that when the focus is on issues that African Americans find are central to their lives (such as exposure to environmental hazards), then they are more likely to become involved in addressing those issues at the local level.

5. One reason for that "marginalization" has to do with what qualifies as being "environmental" within the dominant environmental narrative. The dominant narrative has not considered subsistence fishing and gardening (including urban gardens) as environmental, even though many people, particularly African Americans, engage in these practices. In addition, by carving out spaces that are at once familiar and less visible to the outside world, African Americans can undertake these environmental pursuits in places that are more accessible without having to deal with feelings of exclusion.

6. It should be noted that there is excellent work being done in the humanities that does explore how African Americans have historically thought about nature, including Dungy (2009) and Ruffin (2010).

7. "Conflicted environmental history" refers to how African Americans bear the legacy of slavery, where "American land was a place of punishment and imprisonment for slaves," at the same time recognizing the wilderness as a place of power and knowledge (Blum 2002).

8. The Joneses' story was recently highlighted in Ken Burns's six-part PBS series, "The National Parks: America's Best Idea."

9. While my initial analysis was opportunistic, I strengthened and enriched my initial observations and interpretations through reference to secondary sources in academic and popular publications. This set of events, the coverage by the popular media, and the subsequent reactions are already an icon of race relations in America, and specifically race and environment.

10. My approach to participant observation follows that of Rocheleau (1995) in that it is embedded in a suite of mixed methods and involves a constant iteration with more formal data collection methods for mutual enrichment and maximum effect.

11. I explore this issue, which some call the problem of the "black gatekeeper," in Chapter 5.

12. Throughout this chapter, I discuss diversity in a fairly straightforward and arguably simplistic manner. I am aware of the debates over the merits of diversity. One in particular suggests that "diversity" is just another form of assimilation, and assimilation would mean the loss of African American identity. While I acknowledge the complexity of the diversity question, I have focused this chapter on diversity as a means of inclusion because that is how the NPS and other environmental organizations that I engaged with framed the race and environment discussion.

1. From the official website, *http://www.cherokee-nc.com/index.php?page=62*, sponsored by Eastern Band of the Cherokee Nation. Accessed in 2008.

2. From the National Archives government website http://www.ourdocuments.gov/doc.php?flash=true&doc=26. Treaty of Guadalupe-Hidalgo [Exchange copy], February 2, 1848; Perfected Treaties, 1778–1945; Record Group 11; General Records of the United States Government, 1778–1992; National Archives. Accessed in 2008.

3. In his book, *Understories: The Political Life of Forests in Northern New Mexico*, geographer Jake Kosek explores in depth the impact of the treaty on present-day relationships between federal agencies and Hispano organizations, individuals, and communities in New Mexico.

4. Limerick was speaking about one story in particular that dominated the way in which environmentalists and others spoke about the history of human's relationship with nature in the United States. The story goes something like this: There were three phases: Responses of Fear, Visions of Utilitarian Mastery, and Sentiments of Affection. In Phase 1, Euro-Americans, on setting foot in North America, brought with them the fear that nature and wilderness were scary—the American continent was the big unknown and that was frightening. If forests were scary, they were going to cut the trees and use them to build shelter. In Phase 2, useful animals were hunted, trapped, skins used, meat eaten while "destructive" animals were eliminated all together; land would be cultivated; water used for mills and factories; unused resources would provide homes and jobs. Finally in Phase 3, once we've pushed through the fear and achieved "mastery," it became safe to acknowledge that aspects of nature were very nice and worth preserving. Now we could manage instead of master and feel good about ourselves in the process. And if Nature ever got feisty, we could always go back to "mastery." I have extrapolated Limerick's critique of the limitations of this singular story and applied it to the idea that any singular story about the history of the human/nature relationship can be problematic.

5. Prior involvement of labor unions in the environmental and antinuclear movements of the 1970s was submerged in public discourse and popular media representations.

6. I attended the Second National People of Color Environmental Leadership Summit in Washington, D.C. and heard a panel of mainstream environmental leaders admit that they had done a poor job at creating an ethnically and racially diverse staff and board.

7. It is important to note that African American men and women, especially those in poor and lower-middle-class families, have fished unlicensed with cane poles for food in Florida from long before the twentieth century to the present. Their fishing would have gone unrecorded since most records are obtained from park authorities or licensing documents. In addition, their fishing would have been categorized as subsistence as opposed to recreational fishing. This is another example of statistical invisibility derived from the intersection of race, class, and cultural categories in environmental settings. In addition, the experience of the "great outdoors" for many people is one linked to sustenance, not recreation, and has not been separated into a special recreational category.

8. I also could not find another study, aside from Martin's, that addressed this issue with the sole exception of an article entitled, "The Unbearable Whiteness of Skiing" that focused briefly on how images of ski culture were largely European.

9. The feeling of exclusion was discussed in the 2003 Comprehensive Study of the American Public, conducted by the NPS. According to the study, the visitation rate of African Americans was only 13 percent. In addition, the report states that "African Americans were more than three times likely as whites to believe that park employees gave poor service to visitors, and that parks were uncomfortable places to be for people similar to themselves" (1).

10. My use of the phrase "values of whiteness" is not meant to be an attempt at homogenization. Instead, I seek to highlight the power that "whiteness" as a general term, had (and has) in defining environmental perspectives.

11. After completion of my doctoral research, I was asked to participate on the Second Century Commission and later, through the Department of the Interior, the NPS Advisory Board. In particular, I was asked to chair the committee on relevancy during my four-year term as a board member.

12. "By any means necessary" was a phrase used by Malcolm X during the last year of his life to encourage black people to use any means open to them to achieve freedom and well-being. "We declare our right on this earth to be a man, to be a human being, to be respected as a human being, to be given the rights of a human being in this society, on this earth, in this day, which we intend to bring into existence *by any means necessary*" (1992, 10). While his choice of words implied that violence could be used, I am using this phrase to imagine nonviolent actions that are at once creative, innovative, and revolutionary.

CHAPTER TWO

1. Numerous online articles incited the ire of bloggers on all sides of the conversation. This included "Annie Leibovitz Monkeys Around with LeBron" by Rodgers Cadenhead (March 28, 2008), who raised questions about the photographer's intention; writers from Media Assassin (March 31, 2008) in the article entitled, "Monkey See, Monkey Doo-Doo: How *Vogue* 'Honored' LeBron James by Smearing Black People with White Supremacy & Gorilla Feces," who stated that the photographer Annie Leibovitz and *Vogue* editor Anna Wintour's "blurring of black people and apes" was calculated, and K. R. Kaufman who is considered the first to highlight the comparison on the online community, Democratic Underground. Mainstream media sources such as the Associated Press, the *New York Observer* and ABC News.com also picked up the story.

2. See work by scholars Dorceta Taylor and Dianne Glave.

3. The Smithsonian National Museum of African American History and Culture, slated for completion in 2015, will most likely become the largest.

4. From the Charles H. Wright Museum of African American History website http://www.thewright.org/, sponsored by the museum. Accessed in 2010.

5. "An act to enlarge the powers of the Freedmen's Bureau," 39th Congress, 1st Session, S. 60, in Library of Congress, *A Century of Lawmaking for a New Nation: U.S. Congressional Documents and Debates, 1774–1875*, cited on the Black History website created by Will Moss at http://blackhistory.com/content/60959/40-acres-and-a-mule.

6. There are numerous popular and scholarly accounts of Saartjie Baartman, including works by Deborah Willis, Rachel Holmes, and Clifton Crais.

7. http://www.newworldencyclopedia.org/entry/Civil_rights.

1. Along with the main house, eight slave cabins were also part of Magnolia Plantation's landscape.

2. Interview with Carla Cowles on March 28, 2005, in Montgomery, Alabama.

3. While Cowles wanted to emphasize the need to draw more explicit connections between black residents and the black history that is a part of Magnolia Plantation, she also feels that would deny *all* residents, regardless of their ethnic backgrounds, a more expansive understanding of their history.

4. These links can also be found in the work of present-day storytellers such as Toni Morrison, Maya Angelou, Alice Walker, and J. California Cooper.

5. Evelyn C. White is an African American writer who has written about her experience as a black woman spending time in the wilderness (I explore her experience further in Chapter 6). Henry David Thoreau is an Anglo-American writer who has also written about his experience in the great outdoors. While acknowledging that the two writers lived at different times (White was born in 1954 and Thoreau in 1817), what is similar about them—their feelings about the wilderness, the trees, the solitude of nature—reveals deeper beliefs and perceptions about themselves in relation to place. They come from distinctly different standpoints informed by who they are—she, a black woman, and he, a white man—within the larger context of American society. For Thoreau, the wilderness was a place that was at once inviting and pleasurable. He felt free to walk the land and imagined each place as a "country seat," a place he might live, if he so chose. Conversely, for White, while she recognized the beauty of hiking in a redwood forest or sitting in a boat on a river, she felt fear born out of the memory of other black individuals who had been hunted down and lynched, or forced to hide in the woods (White 1996). While both viewpoints are powerful and contain truths that resonate for many Americans, it is Thoreau's depiction of the wilderness that has the greater influence on how mainstream environmentalists and environmental organizations shape environmental practices.

6. See J. H. Jones, *Bad Blood: The Tuskegee Syphilis Experiment*, rev. ed. (New York: Free Press, 1992).

7. Interview took place on July 29, 2005, on Salt Spring Island, British Columbia.

8. The point is not how one can draw parallels between the "brutal manipulation of nature" by the white man and his treatment of slaves—that's a topic that deserves its own book. (and many have explored this relationship; see McClintock [1995]).

9. I use the terms "enslaved Africans" and "slaves" interchangeably. "Slaves" connotes a dehumanizing description of enslaved black people that I believe accurately reflects how they were thought of, particularly in relation to the environment.

10. By instilling fear—in one case, a white mistress told a young slave that eagles swoop down and take children who play in the woods—white women were able to discourage slaves (particularly women and children) from running away (Blum 2002).

11. The National Underground Railroad Network to Freedom program of the NPS is comprised of diverse historic sites and properties that have some connection to the Underground Railroad.

12. Interviewees had eight potential choices to choose from for the question, "What do you think are the primary issues concerning African American environmental

interaction?" Only those interviewees who gave permission for their names to be used are identified by name.

13. Interview with Leola McCoy on May 12, 2005, in Fort Lauderdale, Florida.

14. Interview with Shelton Johnson on January 25, 2005, at Yosemite National Park, California.

15. Betty Reid Soskin, a prominent community activist, shared her thoughts about the black experience in the creation of park narratives in a talk she gave at the Rosie the Riveter/World War II Home Front National Historic Park, which she helped to create, in Richmond, California.

16. Jim Crow, so named for a "stock character in racist, blackface minstrel shows," mandated that public facilities of all kinds be racially segregated, particularly in the South. In 1896, the U.S. Supreme court in the famous case *Plessy v. Ferguson*, upheld Jim Crow by stating that "separate but equal" was legal (Earle 2000).

17. Billie Holiday made famous a song about lynching called "Strange Fruit."

18. Interview with MaVynee Betsch took place on October 31, 2004, on American Beach, Amelia Island, Florida.

19. The individual, who wished to remain anonymous, was interviewed in 2004 in Florida.

20. In an article in *The Grio*, Rose Hackman reported that African American residents were appalled at the shooting death of Renisha McBride, a young African American woman shot to death in a predominately white neighborhood of Dearborn, Michigan on November 2, 2013. One black resident called Dearborn a sundown town, explaining that black people "know where you should and should not go, where you are safe and where you are not safe" ("Detroit activists demand justice for Renisha McBride," *The Grio*, November 8, 2013, http://act.colorofchange.org/go/3079?t=13&akid=3186.659800.wZT6lT.

21. The individual, who wished to remain anonymous, was interviewed in 2004 in Washington, D.C.

22. Interview took place on January 11, 2004, on Virginia Key Beach, Miami, Florida.

23. Interview took place on October 31, 2004, on American Beach, Amelia Island, Florida.

24. This sentiment was expressed by African Americans and Native Americans at the Summit 2005: Diverse Partners for Environmental Progress. I discuss this workshop more in Chapter 5.

CHAPTER FOUR

1. I use the term "Nature" in this context to represent the public's perception of "Mother Nature" with the connotation of natural phenomena and elements of the natural environment, including weather, water, and land. As the term "Mother Nature" implies, Nature, with a capital "N," is seen as something larger than humanity that can't be controlled, and consequently, has the power to render human beings helpless.

2. What also needs to be acknowledged is the role that media representations of Katrina played in rendering invisible the experiences of people who did not fit the "black/white" framework. John Lie, in his article "The Last Last Wave," wonders where the 20,000 Native Americans said to be living in New Orleans are in the analysis of Hurricane

Katrina, along with the Vietnamese community, said to be the largest concentration of Vietnamese outside of Vietnam. In addition, Lie points to the "racial gloss"—the conflation of others such as Afro-Creoles or Cajuns—into the black/white dichotomy that renders their particular experience of Katrina invisible.

3. Over time, the representations identified by Hall that essentialize black identity have arguably changed in form only. For example, while we no longer see images of black people that caricature big lips and broad noses, we do see images that emphasize black women's big bottoms and suggest that black men are well endowed. In addition, there have been a number of films that show an updated version of the "happy darkie" who works for a white person, like *Driving Miss Daisy*, *The Patriot*, and *Bringing Down the House*. Other characteristics, like laziness and "innate" musical ability, are explored in music videos and mainstream film.

4. In addition, bell hooks, in her book *Black Looks: Race and Representation* (1992), talks about the need to define "blackness" in a particular way in order to legitimize whiteness.

5. An example of a contemporary movie that addresses misrepresentations and stereotypes is Spike Lee's *Bamboozled*.

6. I had the privilege of spending four days with Queen Quet as part of a retreat on St. Helena Island in South Carolina in March of 2005. The retreat focused on the history and culture of the Gullah.

7. I use the term "self-imposed" to acknowledge some degree of agency that individuals possess in making choices. But I want to underscore that for the Gullah, these choices were often made under duress and in the belief that if they are to survive—i.e., get opportunities for self-advancement—they would have to assimilate into American culture in such a way that meant leaving their particular cultural traditions behind.

8. As the old saying goes, history has a way of repeating itself. African American actress Viola Davis was recently nominated (2012) for an Oscar (she did not win) for her portrayal of a domestic living and working in 1960s Mississippi in the critically acclaimed film, *The Help*. She has been praised for both the dignity and humanity she brought to the role.

9. In his new book, *The Persistence of the Color Line: Racial Politics and the Obama Presidency*, Randall Kennedy states that those who felt they would never see a black president indicate "how little they expected of their fellow Americans" (2011, 12). Kennedy points to how white and black Americans were challenged to back Obama in his run up to the presidency.

10. While I could have chosen many movies to discuss, I use the film *The River* to paint a broad brushstroke of how depictions of the environment can implicitly and explicitly exclude certain groups of people from the landscape.

11. I separated the twelve months of the year into four groups of three and labeled each group according to the appropriate season: December, January, and February were winter; March, April, and May were spring; June, July, and August were summer; and September, October, and November were fall. I took each group one at a time, wrote each month on a separate piece of paper, and randomly chose a month from each group out of a hat.

12. *Outside*, November 1992.

13. *Outside* also used the data I collected and reported above, concerning the lack of African American images in their magazine.

14. Interview with Anita McGruder took place on January 12, 2005, in Miami, Florida.

15. Interview with Kris Smith took place on May 6, 2005, in Miami, Florida.

16. The individual, who wished to remain anonymous, was interviewed on February 3, 2005.

17. Interview with John Francis on January 24, 2005, in Point Reyes, California.

18. In 2005, John Francis self-published his story entitled *"Planetwalker": How to Change Your World One Step at a Time*. In 2008, National Geographic republished his book and has generated significant publicity for him and his story.

19. His effort to challenge that norm may get a big boost. I met with John Francis (summer 2006) to get an update on his work. His memoir, *Planetwalker* was picked up by a Hollywood studio. John is presently in negotiations to bring his story to the big screen.

20. Interview with Bill Simmons on January 11, 2005, in Miami, Florida.

21. Interview with Anita Jones on May 3, 2005, in Miami Florida.

22. Interview with Iantha Gantt-Wright by phone on August 15, 2004. We had previously spent time together.

23. *Essence* magazine, July 7, 2004, 196. Interview with my community partner, Audrey Peterman.

24. Based on review of all 192 issues of *Ebony* between 1945 and 1960.

25. Review of brochures was carried out in the media archive for NPS at Harpers Ferry, West Virginia, in February 2005.

26. Based on questionnaires handed out in 2004 and 2005 to park staff at the Everglades, Biscayne, and Big Cypress National Parks.

27. Interview with Carol Daniels in December 2003–January 2004 in Key Biscayne, Florida.

28. Interview with Gayle Hazelwood, assistant superintendent, National Capitol Parks East, on October 9, 2003, in Washington, D.C.

29. You can find Shelton Johnson talking about the buffalo soldiers in the Ken Burn's documentary, *The National Parks: America's Best Idea* or in Johnson's recently published book, *Gloryland*.

30. I was hired on contract as the researcher to gather information and write a historic context study for Biscayne National Park, between September 2004 and September 2005. This piece on Parson Jones is an excerpt from that study. This study was used as a primary source for nominating the Parson Jones site to be listed on the National Register of Historic Places.

31. The story of Israel Lafayette Jones can be found in Ken Burns's documentary *National Parks: America's Best Idea*.

32. Data are from the 1900 Census, Lemon City Precinct 3 and Coconut Grove Precinct 4, Dade County [Fla.], Sheet 35, 285A, pp. 188–89. Delayed Certificate of Birth, filed August 15, 1974. No. 98159.

33. "A History of the Island of Key Biscayne," anonymous, unpublished manuscript (microfiche), p. 112. Original copy at Biscayne National Park.

34. The account is taken from an anonymous article, "250,000 Paid for Island," in the *Miami Herald*, June 13, 1925.

35. *Miami News*, November 15, 1985.

36. "Greater Miami Deaths: Pioneer Fishing Guide" (King Arthur Jones), *Miami News*, February 24, 1966.

37. Tomb, G. 1991. "Man, 92, Shares Bastion of Natural Beauty with Kids," *Miami Herald*, April 17.

38. Oral History Narrative: John Nordt interview with Lancelot Jones at Biscayne National Park, 1990. Original copy at Biscayne National Park Headquarters.

39. As of October 23, 2013, the Jones Family Historic District in Biscayne National Park is listed on the National Register of Historic Places.

40. Along with the Parson Jones site, the NPS is working with the Gullah people in the Carolinas and the black community in American Beach on Amelia Island in Florida to preserve the land and to have visual and textual representations of African American history in both places in their interpretive exhibits.

41. As a participant, I went on a weeklong American Hiking Society outing and took part in a survey distributed by the Kenian Group, organizers working with AHS to improve efforts to increase greater participation.

42. Interview took place on April 5, 2005, in Denver, Colorado.

43. Response given during question-and-answer period following a presentation I gave about my research in February 2006 in Nashville, Tennessee.

44. Interview with Minda Logan on February 4, 2005, in Miami, Florida.

45. Interview with member of the Highway Men in January 2005, in Fort Pierce, Florida.

46. Interview with Anita Jones on May 3, 2005, in Miami, Florida.

47. Interview with Carol Daniels in Key Biscayne, Florida, in January 2004.

48. Interview with Bill Gwaltney in April 2005, in Denver, Colorado.

49. I met with MaVynee Betsch on three separate occasions. This interview took place on October 31, 2004, in American Beach, Florida.

50. Julia Butterfly Hill is an environmental activist who in 1997 lived in a fifteen-hundred-year-old California redwood tree for 738 days to protest the Pacific Lumber Company's attempts to cut it down.

51. I did a participant observation at the Garrison Institute in summer 2002 with forty other "environmentalists" who were invited to attend.

52. Interview with Iantha Gantt-Wright by phone on September 15, 2004. We had previously spent time together in person.

53. Audrey Peterman and her husband Frank published their story in a book entitled, *Legacy on the Land: A Black Couple Discovers Our National Inheritance and Tells Why Every American Should Care*. Audrey Peterman has recently published her second book, *Our True Nature: Finding a Zest for Life in the National Park System*, and is presently writing a daily blog that focuses on different National Park units.

54. Interview with Carla Cowles on March 28, 2005, in Montgomery, Alabama.

55. Interview with Eddy Harris on June 9, 2005, in New York City.

56. The title of his book is *Black and Brown Faces in America's Wild Places*.

57. Interview with Gary Moore on January 16, 2004, in Miami, Florida.

58. The Highwaymen are a group of black painters (all men except for one woman) who painted images of the Florida landscape during the decades of the fifties, sixties, and seventies (though a few still paint today). They were given the name "Highwaymen" because many of them sold their paintings from the back of their cars along the highway.

59. Interviews with five of the Highwaymen and their wives took place on January 12, 2004, in Fort Pierce, Florida.

60. The individual, who chose to remain anonymous, was interviewed on May 12, 2005, in Fort Lauderdale, Florida.

61. The individual, who chose to remain anonymous, was interviewed in 2005 in Fort Lauderdale, Florida.

CHAPTER FIVE

1. Throughout this chapter, I discuss diversity in a fairly straightforward and arguably simplistic manner. However, I am well aware of the debates over the merits of diversity. One in particular suggests that it is just another form of assimilation, and assimilation would mean the loss of African American identity. While I acknowledge the complexity of the issue, I have focused this chapter on diversity as a means of inclusion because that is the way the NPS and other environmental organizations that I engaged with framed the race-and-environment discussion.

2. The O. J. Simpson trial of 1995 and the Los Angeles riots of 1992 are two examples of how racism can spawn divisiveness and violence, respectively. In the case of the Simpson trial (where he was accused of killing his wife Nicole Simpson and her male acquaintance Ronald Goldman in 1994), black and white Americans were divided along color lines— not over the merits of the case, but whether or not Simpson could receive a fair trial because he is black. For African Americans, the belief that the justice system is inherently racist created a chasm of mistrust that no amount of evidence against Simpson could overcome. When Simpson was acquitted, the response to the verdict, particularly from African Americans, "knocked down the floodgates that hold back the waters of racial hostility" (Dyson 2004, 48). The Los Angeles riots of 1992 were the explosive response to the acquittal of four white police offices who had been filmed beating a black man (Rodney King). Almost immediately, fighting and looting broke out in South Central Los Angeles. Over the next six days, "2,383 people were injured, 8,000 arrested, 51 killed, and over 700 businesses were burned" (Bergesen and Herman 1998, 39). California Congresswoman Maxine Waters cited institutionalized racism as one of the root causes of the Rodney King verdict and the Los Angeles riots (Smith 1994).

3. In recent years, the term "environmental justice" has expanded to consider new articulations of injustice on the landscape. Researchers and activists are exploring how to more broadly connect their environmental work with social concerns and address the "geographic dispersion" of environmental justice, a discourse rooted in the United States but one that has found itself realized in different manifestations across the globe (Holifield, Porter, and Walker 2010, 6).

4. According to Marable, individuals from other countries who entered the United States after the Civil Rights Act of 1964 were the primary beneficiaries of affirmative action programs (Marable 2006, 207).

5. The individual, who wished to remain anonymous, was interviewed on April 4, 2005.

6. In his book, *White Guilt: How Blacks and Whites Together Destroyed the Promise of the Civil Rights Era*, Steele discusses his frustration with being reduced to the label of "black conservative" and explores the "forces that created this archetype" and his relationship with this term (2006, 154).

7. Shelby Steele, in an appearance on C-Span, Book TV, April 2, 2006.

8. Naturally, this is not meant to be an exhaustive list.

9. Both bell hooks and Shelby Steele, as black scholars on opposite ends of the political spectrum, point to the danger of *African Americans'* assuming that being black means that there is a common understanding that signifies a similarity in thought, belief, and action. As hooks put it, "why was it impossible to speak of an identity [among African Americans] emerging from a different location?" (hooks 1992, 45). Also see Steele's *White Guilt* (2006, 154–63).

10. A separate piece that addressed the differences in responses would yield an interesting discussion on the impact, if any, these differences had on communal decision making within a predominately black community.

11. Interview with Gentry Davis on October 8, 2003, in Washington, D.C.

12. Interview with Bill Gwaltney, April 4, 2005, in Denver, Colorado.

13. Workshop took place June 12–15, 2005, in Garrison, New York.

14. One consequence of being the only person of color was the implication that I was speaking for all African Americans (and other people of color).

15. The interviewee wished to remain anonymous.

16. The interviewee wished to remain anonymous.

17. Interview with Robert Stanton took place on April 23, 2004, in Washington, D.C.

18. On September 4, 1957, nine black teenagers became the first to test the U.S. Supreme Court's historic *Brown v. Board of Education* decision by attempting to integrate Little Rock Central High School.

19. I experienced how deep these memories can run when my parents visited me in Atlanta in the spring of 2006. We spent an afternoon visiting the Martin Luther King Jr. National Historic Site. As we walked around looking and listening to each of the exhibits that described, through images and voiceovers, Martin Luther King Jr.'s experience, my father suddenly grabbed my arm. I turned to him and asked him if anything was wrong. Laughing self-consciously, he pointed to a "whites only" sign that was part of the exhibit and said that for an instant, he thought we weren't supposed to be there. At seventy-five years old, he was suddenly transported back to a time in his youth, and for a moment it was as real as if it had just happened today.

20. Interview with Ernestine Ray in Fort Lauderdale, Florida, on May 4, 2005.

21. Interview took place on May 20, 2004, in Boston, Massachusetts.

22. Interview took place in January 2004, in Miami, Florida.

23. Interview with Carla Cowles on March 28, 2005, in Montgomery, Alabama. Also, for more on African American experiences in the outdoors, see White (1996) on her time in Oregon.

24. Interview with Audrey Peterman in 2003 in New Hampshire.

25. Interview with Gerrard Jolley on October 8, 2003, in Washington, D.C.

26. Interview with Thirlee Smith in Miami, Florida, on January 18, 2005.

27. The interviewee wished to remain anonymous.

28. Interview with Alan Spears on July 11, 2004, in Leesburg, Virginia.

29. This is, obviously, not an exhaustive list—I focused on these four groups primarily because I have been/am involved with all four.

30. To my knowledge, there have not been any additional gatherings of this particular group, though I believe the original intention was to have an ongoing project.

31. Over the course of two years, I participated in three retreats at the Center for Whole Communities: June and September of 2005, and July of 2006. I am now a faculty member and a board member.

32. The Center for Whole Communities continues to move forward in an effort to remain relevant in the larger "environmental" conversation and to serve a more diverse constituency. In 2011, Peter Forbes stepped down from his role as executive director, and Ginny McGinn stepped in. Both Forbes and McGinn have worked to build a more diverse board, staff, and faculty; to nurture partnerships with environmental organizations focused on diversity; and to expand CWC programs beyond Vermont, to include major urban areas across the United States.

33. I was recently reminded how marginalization can take place even in spaces considered to be highly professional. In her book *No Fear: A Whistleblower's Triumph over Corruption and Retaliation at the EPA*, Marsha Coleman-Adebayo talks about a meeting she attended as only one of two African Americans in a room filled with white males. As she entered the room, her supervisor declared that they would make her an "honorary white man" so that she could join them. Her feelings of humiliation and belittlement served to diminish both her person and her ability to fully participate in the work at hand.

CHAPTER SIX

1. The recent acquittal of George Zimmerman in the shooting death of Trayvon Martin, a young, unarmed African American high school student who was confronted by Zimmerman while in a gated community in Sanford, Florida, on February 26, 2012, further illustrates how these tensions are alive and well.

2. Interview with Eddy Harris took place on June 6, 2005, in New York City.

3. Interview with Bill Gwaltney took place on April 4, 2005, in Denver, Colorado.

4. "Strange Fruit" was originally a poem written by Abel Meeropol, who then set it to music. Billie Holiday released her first recording of the song in 1939.

5. These "green spaces" could include all matter of outside spaces. In December of 2006, six African American teenagers were accused of beating up a white classmate at Jena High School in Louisiana. Charged with attempted murder, the black students began the fight in response to three nooses that had been hung from a tree on the Jena High School playground, considered to be a "white space." The nooses had been hung in response to the presence of a black student who sat under the tree, a space normally "reserved" for white students. For more on this story, visit http://www.democracynow .org/2007/7/10/the_case_of_the_jena_six).

6. Interview with Evelyn C. White on July 29, 2005, on Salt Spring Island, British Columbia.

7. Interview with Palms Barber on May 22, 2009, in Chicago, Illinois.

8. Guyton 2007, vi.

9. John Beardsley, quoted in Guyton 2007, 43.

10. From the Ardea Arts website, http://www.ardeaarts.org/pages/amos.html.

EPILOGUE

1. http://www2.corcoran.org/30americans/.

Works Cited

Agnew, J. A., and J. M. Smith, eds. 2002. *American Space/American Place: Geographies of the Contemporary United States.* New York: Routledge.

Agyeman, J. 1989. "Black People, White Landscape." *Town and Country Planning* 58(12): 336–38.

Agyeman, J., and R. Spooner. 1997. "Ethnicity and the Rural Environment." In *Contested Countryside Cultures: Otherness, Marginalization and Rurality,* edited by P. Cloke and J. Little. London: Routledge.

Alkon, A., and J. Agyeman, eds. 2011. Introduction to *Cultivating Food Justice: Race, Class and Sustainability.* Cambridge, Mass.: MIT Press. 23–46.

Anderson, K. J. 1988. "Cultural Hegemony and the Race-Definition Process in Chinatown, Vancouver: 1880–1980." *Environment and Planning D: Society and Space* 6(2): 127–49.

Anthony, C. 1993. "Carl Anthony Explains Why African-Americans Should Be Environmentalists." In *Major Problems in American Environmental History,* edited by C. Merchant. Lexington, Mass.: D. C. Heath.

Baker, L. D. 1998. *From Savage to Negro: Anthropology and the Construction of Race, 1896–1954.* Berkeley: University of California Press.

Bambara, T. C. 1981. "Some Forward Remarks." In *The Sanctified Church* by Zora Neale Hurston. New York: Marlowe.

Baugh, J. A. 1991. "African-Americans and the Environment: A Review Essay." *Policy Studies Journal* 19(2): 182–91.

Behar, R. 1995. Introduction to *Women Writing Culture,* edited by R. Behar and D. A. Gordon. Berkeley: University of California Press.

Belk, J. 2003. "Big Sky, Open Arms: An Urban Black Family Sheds Some Misgivings on a Trip to Montana." *New York Times,* June 22, Sunday.

Bennett, B. 2002. "A Wild Legacy." *Miami Herald,* July 16, 1E, 3E.

Berenstein, R. J. 1994. "White Heroines and Hearts of Darkness: Race, Gender and Disguise in 1930s Jungle Films." *Film History* 6(3): 314–39.

Bergesen, A., and M. Herman. 1998. "Immigration, Race, and Riot: The 1992 Los Angeles Uprising." *American Sociological Review* 63(1): 39–54.

Bethel, E. R. 1999. *The Roots of African-American Identity: Memory and History in Antebellum Free Communities.* New York: St. Martin's Press.

Blight, D. W. 1994. "W. E. B. Du Bois and the Struggle for American Historical Memory." In *History and Memory in African-American Culture,* edited by G. Fabre and R. O. Meally. New York: Oxford University Press.

Bloom, L. 1993. *Gender on Ice: American Ideologies of Polar Expeditions*. Minneapolis: University of Minnesota Press.

Blum, E. D. 2002. "Power, Danger, and Control: Slave Women's Perceptions of Wilderness in the Nineteenth Century. *Women's Studies* 31(2): 247–65.

Bogle, D. 1992. *Toms, Coons, Mulattoes, Mammies and Bucks: An Interpretive History of Blacks in American Films*. New York: Continuum.

Bonnet, A. 2000. *White Identities: Historical and International Perspectives*. New York: Prentice Hall.

Boucher, N. 1991. "Smart as Gods: Can We Put the Everglades Back Together Again?" *Wilderness* 55(195): 11–21.

Boyd, V. 2003. *Wrapped in Rainbows: The Life of Zora Neale Hurston*. New York: Scribner.

Braun, B. 2003. "On the Raggedy Edge of Risk: Articulations of Race and Nature after Biology." In *Race, Nature and the Politics of Difference*, edited by D. Moore, J. Kosek and A. Pandian. Durham, N.C.: Duke University Press.

Brundage, W. F. 2000. "No Deed but Memory." In *Where These Memories Grow: History, Memory, and Southern Identity*. Chapel Hill: University of North Carolina Press.

Bryant, B. 1995. *Environmental Justice: Issues, Policies and Solutions*. Washington, D.C.: Island Press.

Bullard, R. 1995. *Dumping in Dixie: Race, Class and Environmental Quality*. Boulder, Colo.: Westview Press.

Bush, G. 2006. "Politicized Memories in the Struggle for Miami's Virginia Key Beach." In *To Love the Wind and the Rain: African Americans and Environmental History*, edited by D. Glave and M. Stoll. Pittsburgh: University of Pittsburgh Press.

Camacho, D. E. 1998. *Environmental Injustices, Political Struggles: Race, Class, and the Environment*. Durham, N.C.: Duke University Press.

Carney, J. A. 2001. *Black Rice: The African Origins of Rice Cultivation in the Americas*. Cambridge, Mass.: Harvard University Press.

Chang, I. 2004. *The Chinese in America: A Narrative History*. New York: Penguin.

Clifton, L. 2004. *Mercy*. Rochester, N.Y.: BOA Editions.

Cloke, P., and J. Little, eds. 1997. *Contested Countryside Cultures: Otherness, Marginalization and Rurality*. London: Routledge.

Cole, L. W., and S. R. Foster. 2001. *From the Ground Up: Environmental Racism and the Rise of the Environmental Justice Movement*. New York: New York University Press.

Cole, O. 1999. *The African-American Experience in the Civilian Conservation Corps*. Gainesville: University Press of Florida.

Coleman, A. G. 1996. "The Unbearable Whiteness of Skiing: Racial Discrimination in Ski Resort Employment." *Pacific Historical Review* 65(4): 583–615.

Collins, P. H. 2000. *Black Feminist Thought: Knowledge, Consciousness, and the Politics of Empowerment*. 2nd ed. New York: Routledge.

Cose, E. 1993. *The Rage of the Privileged Class: Why Are Middle-Class Blacks Angry? Why Should America Care?* New York: Harper Perennial.

Coser, L. 1992. *On Collective Memory*. Chicago: University of Chicago Press.

Cronon, W., ed. 1996. *Uncommon Ground: Rethinking the Human Place in Nature*. New York: W. W. Norton.

Cruikshank, J. 1998. *The Social Life of Stories: Narrative and Knowledge in the Yukon Territory*. Vancouver: UBC Press.

Daniels, R. 2002. "Racism: Looking Forward, Looking Back." In *Race and Resistance: African Americans in the 21st Century*, edited by H. Boyd. Boston: South End Press.

Da Vasquez, S. T. 2001, "A Theology of Life, Death, and Transformation." In *Sites of Memory: Perspectives on Architecture and Race*, edited by Craig E. Barton. New York: Princeton Architectural Press.

Day, K. 1999. "Embassies and Sanctuaries: Women's Experiences of Race and Fear in Public Space." *Environment and Planning D: Society and Space* 17(3): 307–28.

DeGruy Leary, J. 2005. *Post Traumatic Slave Syndrome: America's Legacy of Enduring Injury and Healing*. Portland, Ore.: Uptone Press.

Delaney, D. 2002. "The Space That Race Makes." *Professional Geographer* 54(1): 6–14

DeLuca, K. 1999. "The Shadow of Whiteness: The Consequences of Constructions of Nature in Environmental Politics." In *Whiteness: The Communication of Social Identity*, edited by T. K. Nakayama and J. N. Martin. Thousand Oaks, Calif.: Sage.

DeLuca, K., and A. Demo. 2001. "Imagining Nature and Erasing Class and Race: Carleton Watkins, John Muir, and the Construction of the Wilderness." *Environmental History* 6(4): 541–60.

Deming, A. H., and L. E. Savoy, eds. 2011. *The Colors of Nature: Culture, Identity and the Natural World.* 2nd ed. Minneapolis: Milkweed Press.

Dickerson, D. J. 2004. *The End of Blackness: Returning the Souls of Black Folk to Their Rightful Owners*. New York: Pantheon Books.

Dilsaver, L. M. 1994. *America's National Park System: The Critical Documents*. New York: Rowman and Littlefield Publishers.

Dixon, M. 1987. *Ride Out the Wilderness: Geography and Afro-American Literature*. Chicago: University of Illinois Press.

Dominy, M. D. 1997. "The Alpine Landscape in Australian Mythologies of Ecology and Nation." In *Knowing Your Place: Rural Identity and Cultural Hierarchy*, edited by B. Ching and G. Creed. London: Routledge.

Douglas, M. S. 1997. *The Everglades: River of Grass*. 50th anniversary ed. Sarasota, Fla.: Pineapple Press.

Du Bois, W. E. B. 1995. *The Philadelphia Negro: A Social Study*. Philadelphia: University of Pennsylvania Press.

DuBuys, W. 1985. *Enchantment and Exploitation: The Life and Hard Times of a New Mexico Mountain Range*. Albuquerque: University of New Mexico Press.

Dunaway, F. 2005. *Natural Visions: The Power of Images in American Environmental Reform*. Chicago: University of Chicago Press.

Duncan, J. 1993. "Sites of Representation: Place, Time and the Discourse of the Other." In *Place, Culture, Representation*, edited by J. Duncan and D. Ley. London: Routledge.

Dungy, C. 2009. *Black Nature: Four Centuries of African American Nature Poetry*. Athens: University of Georgia Press.

Dunn, M. 1997. *Black Miami in the Twentieth Century*. Gainesville: University Press of Florida.

Duveen, G., and S. Moscovici, eds. 2001. *Social Representations: Essays in Social Psychology*. New York: New York University Press.

Dwyer, O. J. 1997. "Geographical Research about African-Americans: A Survey of Journals, 1911–1995." *Professional Geographer* 49(4): 441–51.

Dyson, M. E. 1999. "Race and the Public Intellectual: A Conversation with Michael Eric Dyson." In *Race, Rhetoric and the Postcolonial*, edited by G. A. Olson and L. Worsham. New York: State University of New York Press.

———. 2006. *Come Hell or High Water: Hurricane Katrina and the Color of Disaster*. New York: Basic Civitas Books.

Earle, J. 2000. *The Routledge Atlas of African-American History*. New York: Routledge.

Edmondson, D. 2006. *Black and Brown Faces in America's Wild Places*. Cambridge, Minn.: Adventure Publications.

Elder, G., J. Wolch, and J. Emel. 1998. "Race, Place and the Bounds of Humanity." *Society and Animals* 6(2): 183–202.

Ellis, C., and R. Ginsburg, eds. 2010. Introduction to *Cabin, Quarter, Plantation: Architecture and Landscapes of North American Slavery*. New Haven: Yale University Press.

Erdmans, M. P. 2007. "The Personal Is Political, but Is It Academic? Women's Life Stories and Oral Histories." *Journal of American Ethnic History* 26(4): 7–23.

Ewen, S., and E. Ewen. 2008. *Typecasting: On the Arts and Sciences of Human Inequality*. New York: Seven Stories Press.

Eyerman, R. 2001. *Cultural Trauma: Slavery and the Formation of African American Identity*. New York: Cambridge University Press.

Fentress, J., and C. Wickham. 1992. *Social Memory*. Oxford: Blackwell.

Ferguson, L. 1992. *Uncommon Ground: Archeology and Early African America, 1650–1800*. Washington, D.C.: Smithsonian Institution Press.

Finley, C. 2001. "The Door of (No) Return." *Common Place* 1(4): 1–4.

Finney, C. 2003. "Can't See the Black Folks for the Trees." In *Voices for a New Century*, edited by C. Faulkner and S. Weir. Boston: Allyn & Bacon.

Finney, C., and L. Fraser. 2011. "Status Report to the National Parks Board."

Floyd, M. 1999. "Race, Ethnicity, and Use of the National Park System." *Social Science Research Review* 1(2): 1–24.

Franklin, J. H., and L. Schweninger. 1999. *Runaway Slaves: Rebels on the Plantation*. New York: Oxford University Press.

Frazier, J. W., F. Margai, and E. Tettie-Fio. 2003. *Race and Place: Equity Issues in Urban America*. Boulder, Colo.: Westview Press.

Friedman, S. S. 1995. "Beyond White and Other: Relationality and Narratives of Race in Feminist Discourse." *Signs* 21(1): 1–49.

Gelobter, M., M. Dorsey, L. Fields, T. Goldtooth, A. Mendiratta, R. Moore, R. Morello-Frosch, P. Shepard, and G. Torres. 2005. "The Soul of Environmentalism: Rediscovering Transformational Politics in the 21st Century." Commonweal Institute. Progressive Roundtable. http://www.rprogress.org/soul/soul.pdf.

Gilbert, M. R. 1998. "'Race,' Space, and Power: The Survival Strategies of Working Poor Women." *Annals of the Association of American Geographers* 88(4): 595–621.

Gilmore, R. W. 2002. "Fatal Couplings of Power and Difference: Notes on Racism and Geography." *Professional Geographer* 54(1): 15–24.

Gilroy, P. 1993. *Small Acts: Thoughts on the Politics of Black Cultures*. London: Serpent's Tail.

Giltner, S. 2006. "Slave Hunting and Fishing in the Antebellum South." In *To Love the Wind and the Rain: African Americans and Environmental History*, edited by D. Glave and M. Stoll. Pittsburgh: University of Pittsburgh Press.

Ginsburg, R. 2010. "Escaping through a Black Landscape." In *Cabin, Quarter, Plantation: Architecture and Landscapes of North American Slavery*, edited by C. Ellis and R. Ginsburg. New Haven: Yale University Press.

Glave, D., and M. Stoll, eds. 2006. *To Love the Wind and the Rain: African Americans and Environmental History*. Pittsburgh: University of Pittsburgh Press.

Goldsmith, J. 1994. "Designing for Diversity." *National Parks Conservation Association Magazine* 20 (May/June): 20.

Goodwine, M., ed. 1998. *The Legacy of Ibo Landing: Gullah Roots of African-American Culture*. Atlanta, Ga.: Clarity Press.

Gore, A. 2006. "The Moment of Truth." *Vanity Fair*, May. 170–99.

Grandison, K. I. 1996. "Landscapes of Terror: A Reading of Tuskegee's Historic Campus." In *The Geography of Identity*, edited by P. Yaeger. Ann Arbor: University of Michigan Press.

Grier, W. H., and P. M. Cobbs. 1968. *Black Rage*. New York: Bantam Books.

Griffin, F. J., and C. J. Fish, eds. 1998. *A Stranger in the Village: Two Centuries of African-American Travel Writing*. Boston: Beacon Press.

Guinier, L., and G. Torres, eds. 2002. *The Miner's Canary: Enlisting Race, Resisting Power, Transforming Democracy*. Cambridge, Mass.: Harvard University Press.

Guthman, J. 2011. *Weighing In: Obesity, Food Justice and the Limits of Capitalism*. Berkeley: University of California Press.

Guyton, Tyree. 2007. *Connecting the Dots: Tyree Guyton's Heidelberg Project*. Detroit, Mich.: Wayne State University Press.

Gwaltney, John Langston. 1993. *Drylongso: A Self-Portrait of Black America*. New York: New Press.

Hall, S. 1996. "New Ethnicities." In *Critical Dialogues in Cultural Studies*, edited by D. Morley and K. Chen. London: Routledge.

———, ed. 1997. *Representation: Cultural Representations and Signifying Practices*. London: Sage.

Haraway, D. 1989. *Primate Visions: Gender, Race, and Nature in the World of Modern Science*. New York: Routledge.

———. 1991. "Situated Knowledges." In *Simians, Cyborgs and Women: The Reinvention of Nature*. New York: Routledge.

Harris, C. 1993. "Whiteness as Property." *Harvard Law Review* 106(8): 277.

Harris, E. L. 1988. *Mississippi Solo: A Memoir*. New York: Henry Holt.

Harris-Perry, M. V. 2011. *Sister Citizen: Shame, Stereotypes, and Black Women in America*. New Haven: Yale University Press.

Heart and Mind of Environmental Leadership workshop. 2005. Draft proposal.

Hendricks, R. L. 2006. "A Brief History of African Americans and Forests." International Programs, U.S. Forest Service. http://www.fs.fed.us/global/wsnew/fs_history.htm.

Hoffman, D. 1997. "Whose Home on the Range?: Finding Room for Native Americans, African Americans, and Latino Americans in the Revisionist Western." *MELUS* 22(2): 45–59.

Holifield, R., M. Porter, and G. Walker, eds. 2010. *Spaces of Environmental Justice*. Hoboken, N.J.: Wiley-Blackwell.

Holland, J. W. 2002. *Black Recreation: A Historical Perspective*. Chicago: Burnham.

hooks, b. 1992. *Black Looks: Race and Representation*. Boston: Southend Press.

———. 1994. *Outlaw Culture: Resisting Representations*. London: Routledge.

Huffington Post. 2010. "Glenn Beck Compares Obama's America to Planet of the Apes." Video, http://www.huffingtonpost.com/2010/08/07/glenn-beck-compares-obama_n_674591.html

Hurston, Z. N. 1981. *The Sanctified Church*. New York: Marlowe.

Irwin-Zarecka, I. 1994. *Frames of Remembrance: The Dynamics of Collective Memory*. New Brunswick, N.J.: Transaction.

Jackson, P. 1994. "Racism." In *The Dictionary of Human Geography*, edited by R. J. Johnston, D. Gregory, and D. M. Smith. Oxford: Blackwell.

———. 1998. "Construction of 'Whiteness' in the Geographical Imagination." *Area* 30(2): 99–106.

Jacoby, K. 1997. "Class and Environmental History: Lessons from the War in the Adirondacks." *Environmental History* 2(3): 324–42.

Johnson, C., and J. M. Bowker. 2004. "African American Wildland Memories." *Environmental Ethics* 26(1): 57–74.

Johnson, C. Y., J. M. Bowker, D. B. K. English, and D. Worthen. 1997. "Theoretical Perspectives of Ethnicity and Outdoor Recreation: A Review and Synthesis of African-American Participation." In *General Technical Report SRS-11*: U.S. Department of Agriculture, Forest Service.

Johnson, C. Y., and J. McDaniel. 2006. "Turpentine Negro." In *To Love the Wind and the Rain: African Americans and Environmental History*, edited by D. Glave and M. Stoll. Pittsburgh: University of Pittsburgh Press.

Jones, V. 2008. *The Green Collar Economy: How One Solution Can Fix Our Two Biggest Problems*. New York: Harper.

Kahn, P. H. 2001. *The Human Relationship with Nature: Development and Culture*. Cambridge, Mass.: MIT Press.

Kaufman, P. W. 1996. *National Parks and the Woman's Voice: A History*. Albuquerque: University of New Mexico Press.

Kennedy, R. 2011. *The Persistence of the Color Line: Racial Politics and the Obama Presidency*. New York: Pantheon.

Klotman, P. R., and J. K. Cutler, eds. 1999. *Struggles for Representations: African-American Documentary Film and Video*. Bloomington: Indiana University Press.

Kobayashi, A., and L. Peake. 1994. "Unnatural Discourse: 'Race' and Gender in Geography." *Gender, Place and Culture* 1:225–44.

Kook, R. 1998. "The Shifting Status of African-Americans in the American Collective Identity." *Journal of Black Studies* 29(2): 154–78.

Kosek, Jake. 2006. *Understories: The Political Life of Forests in Northern New Mexico*. Durham, N.C.: Duke University Press.

Krech, S. 1999. *The Ecological Indian: Myth and History*. New York: W. W. Norton.

Kureishi, H. 2012. "The Art of Distraction." *New York Times*, February 18. http://www.nytimes.com/2012/02/19/opinion/sunday/the-art-of-distraction.html.

Kurtz, H. 2010. "Acknowledging the Racial State: An Agenda for Environmental Justice Research." In *Spaces of Environmental Justice*, edited by R. Holifield, M. Porter, and G. Walker. Hoboken, N.J.: Wiley-Blackwell.

Laroche, C. 2010. "The Balance Principle: Slavery, Freedom, and the Formation of the Nation." In *Cabin, Quarter, Plantation: Architecture and Landscapes of North American Slavery*, edited by C. Ellis and R. Ginsburg. New Haven: Yale University Press.

"Letters to the Editor." 1994. *National Parks Conservation Association Magazine.* September/October.

———. 1995. *National Parks Conservation Association Magazine.* January/February.

Lie, J. 2002. "The Last Last Wave." *Du Bois Review* 3(1): 233–38.

Limerick, P. N. 2000. *Something in the Soil: Legacies and Reckonings in the New West.* New York: W. W. Norton.

Litwack, L. F. 2004. "Hellhounds." In *Without Sanctuary*, edited by J. Allen, H. Als, J. Lewis, and L. Litwack. Albuquerque: Twin Palms.

Loewen, J. W. 2005. *Sundown Towns: A Hidden Dimension of American Racism.* New York: New Press.

Lovett, F. 1998. *National Parks: Rights and the Common Good.* Lanham, Md.: Rowman and Littlefield.

Lowenthal, D. 2000. "Nature and Morality from George Perkins Marsh to the Millennium." *Journal of Historical Geography* 26(1): 3–27.

Lucero, B. 2009. "Talking Points: Las Trampas Land Grant Association." http://www.lucerito.net/documents/TalkingPoints18Apr2009.pdf.

MacEachern, A. 1995. "Civil Rights: Why Martin Luther King Didn't Spend His Summer Vacation in Canada, 1960; the U.S. Civil Rights Leader Was Turned Away by a Resort in New Brunswick." Toronto *Globe and Mail*, January 14.

A Man Named Pearl. 2008. Documentary film directed by Scott Galloway and Brent Pierson. Susie Films and Tentmakers Entertainment.

Manring, M. M. 1998. *Slave in a Box: The Strange Career of Aunt Jemima.* Charlottesville: University Press of Virginia.

Marable, M. 2006. *Living Black History: How Reimagining the African-American Past Can Remake America's Racial Future.* New York: Basic Civitas Books.

———. 2011. "Introduction: The Prism of Race." In *Beyond Boundaries: The Manning Marable Reader*, edited by R. Rickford. Boulder, Colo.: Paradigm.

Martin, D. C. 2004. "Apartheid in the Great Outdoors: American Advertising and the Reproduction of a Racialized Outdoor Leisure Identity." *Journal of Leisure Research* 36(4): 513–35.

McClintock, A. 1995. *Imperial Leather: Race, Gender and Sexuality in the Colonial Conquest.* London: Routledge.

McElroy, C. J. 1997. *A Long Way from St. Louie: Travel Memoir.* Minneapolis: Coffee House Press.

Measures of Health. 2005. Center for Whole Communities. Fayston, Vt.: N.p.

Meeker, J. W. 1984. "Red, White, and Black in National Parks." In *On Interpretation: Sociology for Interpreters of Natural and Cultural History*, edited by G. Machlis and D. R. Field. Corvallis: Oregon State University Press.

Mellon, J., ed. 1988. *Bullwhip Days: The Slaves Remember.* New York: Avon.

Merchant, C. 1989. *Ecological Revolutions: Nature, Gender, and Science in New England.* Chapel Hill: University of North Carolina Press.

———. 1990. "Gender and Environmental History." *Journal of American History* 76(4): 1117–21.

———. 2003. "Shades of Darkness: Race and Environmental History." *Environmental History* 8(3): 380–94.

Metress, C. 2002. *The Lynching of Emmett Till: A Documentary Narrative.* Charlottesville: University Press of Virginia.

Miller, V., M. Hallstein, and S. Quass. 1996. "Feminist Politics and Environmental Justice." In *Feminist Political Ecology: Global Issues and Local Experiences,* edited by D. Rocheleau, B. Thomas-Slaytor and E. Wangari. London: Routledge.

Mitchell, O., and N. Smith. 1999. "Bringing in Race." *Professional Geographer* 42(2): 232–34.

Mohai, P. 1992. *Race and the Incidence of Environmental Hazards: A Time for Discourse.* Boulder, Colo.: Westview Press.

———. 2003. "Dispelling Old Myths." *Environment* 45(5): 11–26.

Mohl, R. A. 1991. "The Settlement of Blacks in South Florida." In *Association of American Geographers,* edited by T. D. Boswell. Tallahassee, Fla.: Rose Press.

Moore, D. S., J. Kosek, and A. Pandian. 2003. *Race, Nature, and the Politics of Difference.* Durham, N.C.: Duke University Press.

Mormino, G. R. 2005. *Land of Sunshine, State of Dreams: A Social History of Modern Florida.* Gainesville: University Press of Florida.

Morrison, T. 2008. *What Moves at the Margins: Selected Nonfiction.* Jackson: University Press of Mississippi.

Moscovici, S. 2001. *Social Representations: Explorations in Social Psychology.* New York: New York University Press.

Myers, J. 2005. *Converging Stories: Race, Ecology, and Environmental Justice in American Literature.* Athens: University of Georgia Press.

Nagar, R. 1998. "Communal Discourses, Marriage, and the Politics of Gendered Social Boundaries among South Asian Immigrants in Tanzania." *Gender, Place and Culture* 5(2): 117–39.

Nash, R. 1982. *Wilderness and the American Mind.* 3rd ed. New Haven, Conn.: Yale University Press.

Nast, H. 1999. "'Sex,' 'Race,' and Multiculturalism: Critical Consumption and the Politics of Course Evaluations." *Journal of Geography in Higher Education* 23(1): 102–15.

Neal, S., and J. Agyeman. 2006. *The New Countryside?: Ethnicity, Nation and Exclusion in Contemporary Rural Britain.* Bristol, UK: Policy Press.

Oelschlaeger, M. 1991. *The Idea of Wilderness: From Prehistory to the Age of Ecology.* New Haven: Yale University Press.

Ogbar, J. O. G. 2004. *Black Power: Radical Politics and African American Identity.* Baltimore: Johns Hopkins University Press.

Outka, P. 2008. *Race and Nature: From Transcendentalism to the Harlem Renaissance.* New York: Palgrave Macmillan.

Penrose, J. 2003. "When All Cowboys Were Indians: The Nature of Race in an All-Indian Rodeo." *Annals of the Association of American Geographers* 93(3): 687–705.

Peterman, A. 2005. "Continental Divide." In *National Parks Conservation Association Magazine* 79(4): 17–19.

Philipp, S. F. 1995. "Race and Leisure Constraints." *Leisure Sciences* 17(2): 109–20.

Pollard, I. 2004. *Postcards Home*. London: Chris Boot.

Principles of Working Together Working Group. 2002. Document submitted at the People of Color Environmental Leadership Summit in Washington, D.C., October 26.

Pulido, L. 1997. "Community, Place, and Identity." In *Thresholds in Feminist Geography*, edited by J. P. Jones III, H. J. Nast, and S. M. Roberts. New York: Rowman and Littlefield.

———. 2000. "Rethinking Environmental Racism: White Privilege and Urban Development in Southern California." *Annals of the Association of American Geographers* 90(1): 12–40.

———. 2002. "Reflections on a White Discipline." *Professional Geographer* 54(1): 42–49.

Radcliff, S., and S. Westwood. 1993. "Gender, Racism, and the Politics of Identities in Latin America." In *Viva: Women and Popular Protest in Latin America*, edited by S. Radcliffe and S. Westwood. London: Routledge.

Roberts, N. 2004. "Diversity Connections: A National Inventory." Department of the Interior *NPS* 2(winter): 2–16.

Roberts, N., and E. B. Drogin. 1996. "The Outdoor Recreation Experience: Factors Affecting Participation of African-American Women." In *Women's Voices in Experiential Education*, edited by K. Warren. Dubuque, Iowa: Kendall/Hunt Publishing.

Rocheleau, D., and R. Slocum. 1995. "Participation in Context: Key Questions." In *Power, Process, and Participation: Tools for Change*, edited by R. Slocum, L. Wichita, D. Rocheleau and B. Thomas-Slaytor. London: Intermediate Technology.

Rogers, P. A. 1994. "Hard Core Poverty." In *Picturing Us: African-American Identity in Photography*. New York: New Press.

Ruffin, Kimberly N. 2010. *Black on Earth: African American Ecoliteracy Traditions*. Athens: University of Georgia Press.

Runte, A. 1997. *National Parks: The American Experience*. Lincoln: University of Nebraska Press.

Rydell, R. W. 1984. *All the World's a Fair: Visions of Empire at American International Expositions, 1876–1916*. Chicago: University of Chicago Press.

Rymer, R. 1998. *American Beach: A Saga of Race, Wealth, and Memory*. New York: Harper Collins.

Samuels, A., and J. Adler. 2010. "The Reinvention of the Reverend." *Newsweek*, August 2, 2010.

Sayers, D. 2005. "Diasporan Exiles in the Great Dismal Swamp: 1630–1860." *Transforming Anthropology* 14(1): 10–20.

Schama, S. 1995. *Landscape and Memory*. New York: Vintage Books.

Shackel, P. 2003. *Memory in Black and White: Race, Commemoration, and the Post-Bellum Landscape*. New York: Altamira Press.

Shein, R. 2002. "Race, Racism, and Geography: Introduction." *Professional Geographer* 54(1): 1–5.

Shelby, T. 2005. *We Who Are Dark: The Philosophical Foundations of Black Solidarity*. Cambridge, Mass.: Harvard University Press.

Sheppard, J. A. C. 1995. "The Black-White Environmental Concern Gap: An Examination of Environmental Paradigms. *Journal of Environmental Education* 26(2): 24–25.

Sibley, David. 1995. *Geographies of Exclusion: Society and Difference in the West*. London: Routledge.

Simpson, B. 1990. *The Great Dismal Swamp: A Carolinian's Swamp Memoir*. Chapel Hill: University of North Carolina Press.

Simpson, J. 2002. *Yearning for the Land: A Search for the Importance of Place*. New York: Pantheon.

Smedley, A. 1993. *Race in North America: Origin and Evolution of a Worldview*. Boulder, Colo.: Westview Press.

Smith, A. D. 1994. *Twilight: Los Angeles, 1992*. New York: Anchor Books.

Smith, D. L. 1996. "African Americans, Writing and Nature." In *American Nature Writers*, edited by J. Elder. Farmington Hills, MI: Gale Group.

Smith, K. 2004. "Black Agrarianism and the Foundations of Black Environmental Thought." *Environmental Ethics* 26(3): 267–86.

———. 2007. *African American Environmental Thought: Foundations*. Lawrence: University Press of Kansas.

Soja, E., and B. Hooper. 1993. "The Spaces That Difference Makes: Some Notes on the Geographical Margins of the New Cultural Politics." In *Place and the Politics of Identity*, edited by M. Keith and S. Pile. Routledge: London.

Solop, F. I., K. K. Hagen, and D. Ostergren. 2003. "Ethnic and Racial Diversity of National Park System Visitors and Non-Visitors: Technical Report." Flagstaff: Northern Arizona University.

Spence, M. D. 1999. *Dispossessing the Wilderness: Indian Removal and the Making of the National Parks*. New York: Oxford University Press.

Staeheli, L. A., and P. M. Martin. 2000. "Spaces for Feminism in Geography." *Annals of the American Academy of Political and Social Science* 571 (September): 135–50.

Steele, S. 2006. *White Guilt: How Blacks and Whites Together Destroyed the Promise of the Civil Rights Era*. New York: Harper Collins.

Stein, R. 1997. *Shifting the Ground: American Women Writers' Revisions of Nature: Explorations in Ecocriticism*. Charlottesville: University Press of Virginia.

Stein, S. 2009. "*New York Post* Chimp Cartoon Compares Stimulus Author to Dead Primate." February 18. *Huffington Post* online.

"Steps for the Future." 2005. Summit Report: Diverse Partners for Environmental Progress. http://www.environmentaldiversity.org/documents/Summit05finalreport.pdf.

Stewart, M. 2006. "Slavery and the Origins of African American Environmentalism." In *To Love the Wind and the Rain: African Americans and Environmental History*, edited by D. Glave and M. Stoll. Pittsburgh: University of Pittsburgh Press.

Strait, Kevin. 2004. "Presenting Race and Slavery at Historic Sites, Arlington House, Robert E. Lee National Memorial." Report prepared for the National Park Service and the Center for the Study of Public Culture and Public History of the George Washington University.

Sullivan, Robert. 2008. "LeBron James and Gisele Bündchen: Dream Team." *Vogue*, April.

Sundberg, J. 2002. "Imperial Imaginaries of Nature and 'Race' in the Maya Biosphere Reserve, Guatemala." Paper read at 98th Annual Meeting of the Association of American Geographers, March 19–23, at Los Angeles, Calif.

Sze, J. 2006. *Noxious New York: The Racial Politics of Urban Health and Environmental Justice*. Boston: MIT Press.

Taylor, D. E. 1989. "Blacks and the Environment: Toward an Explanation of the Concern and Action Gap between Blacks and Whites." *Environment and Behavior* 21(2): 175–205.

———. 1997. "American Environmentalism: The Role of Race, Class and Gender in Shaping Activism 1820-1995." *Race, Gender and Class* 5(1): 16-62.

Thompson, G. 2000. "Reaping What Was Sown on the Old Plantation." *New York Times,* June 22.

Toila-Kelly, D. 2004. "Landscape, Race, and Memory: Biographical Mapping of the Routes of British Asian Landscape Values." *Landscape Research* 29(3): 277-92.

Trethewey, N. 2010. "Our Loss, through the Eye of the Storm." *New York Times,* September 29.

Twine, F. W. 2000. "Racial Ideologies and Racial Methodologies." In *Racing Research, Researching Race: Methodological Dilemmas in Critical Race Studies,* edited by F. W. Twine and J. W. Warren. New York: New York University Press.

U.S. Department of the Interior. 2002. *National Parks Diversity Initiatives Report.* Washington, D.C.

Vale, T. R. 1995. *The American Wilderness: Reflections on Nature Protection in the United States.* Charlottesville: University Press of Virginia.

Virden, R. J., and G. J. Walker. 1999. "Ethnic/Racial and Gender Variations among Meanings Given to, and Preferences for, the Natural Environment." *Leisure Sciences* 21(3): 219-39.

Walker, C. 1994. "Gazing Colored: A Family Album." In *Picturing Us: African-American Identity in Photography.* New York: New Press.

West, C. 2001. *Race Matters.* New York: Vintage Books.

West, P. 1993. "The Tyranny of Metaphor: Interracial Relations, Minority Recreation, and the Wildland-Urban Interface." In *Culture, Conflict, and Communication in the Wildland-Urban Interface,* edited by A. W. Ewert, D. J. Chavez, and A. W. Magill. Boulder, Colo.: Westview Press.

White, E. C. 1996. "Black Women and the Wilderness." In *Names We Call Home: Autobiography on Racial Identity,* edited by B. Thompson and S. Tyagi. London: Routledge.

Wideman, J. E. 2001. Foreword. In *Every Tongue Got to Confess: Negro Folk Tales From the Gulf States,* edited by Carla Kaplan. New York: Harper Collins.

Williams-Forson, P. A. 2006. *Building Houses out of Chicken Legs: Black Women, Food, and Power.* Chapel Hill: University of North Carolina Press.

Wilson, B. 2000. *Race and Place in Birmingham.* Lanham, Md.: Rowman and Littlefield.

Wilson, M. 2001. "Between Rooms: Spaces of Memory at the National Civil Rights Museum." In *Sites of Memory: Perspectives on Architecture and Race.* New York: Princeton Architectural Press.

Wohlforth, C. 2010. "Conservation and Eugenics: The Environmental Movement's Dirty Little Secret." *Orion Magazine* July/August, 22-28.

Woods, C. 1998. *Development Arrested: Race, Power, and Blues in the Mississippi Delta.* New York: Verso.

Worster, D. 1990. "Transformations of the Earth: Toward an Agroecological Perspective in History." *Journal of American History* 76(4): 1087-1106.

———. 1993. *The Wealth of Nature: Environmental History and the Ecological Imagination.* New York: Oxford University Press.

X, Malcolm. 1992. *By Any Means Necessary: Malcolm X Speeches and Writings.* New York: Pathfinder Press.

Acknowledgments

There are many people, places, moments, and spirits to thank. What a privilege it has been to be able to spend time building new relationships, hearing stories, and doing work and research that allows me the opportunity to better understand the relationships we have with each other and this earth on which we live.

I would like to thank the department of geography at Clark University, for giving me the opportunity to pursue this project. The faculty and the students were simply outstanding. In particular, I want to thank my graduate advisor, Dianne Rocheleau, who wholeheartedly supported the idea for this research and believed that I could do it. Her tenacity and her integrity in the way she does her work set the bar high, and I continue to follow her example. I also want to thank my teachers and colleagues Susan Hanson, Billie Turner, and Dianne Glave. A special shout out to some of my Clark peers who continue to do amazing things in the world: Trina Hamilton, Robin Roth, Mazen Labban, Laura Schneider, Alice Hovorka, Thomas Ponniah, Jackie Vadjunec, Daniel Niles, and Susannah McCandless. You rock.

I want to thank the funders who made it possible for me to pay the rent while doing my research: The Society of Women Geographers Pruitt Fellowship, the Ford Foundation Community Forestry Fellowship, and the Canon National Parks Science Scholars Program. I also want to thank the Division of Social Sciences in the College of Letters and Science at the University of California, Berkeley, for awarding me an Abigail Reynolds Hodgens Publications Grant and the Agricultural Experimental Station Merit Award so that I could complete my book.

In addition, thank you to the Department of Environmental Studies at Wellesley College for providing me with a Mellon Postdoctoral Fellowship so that I could continue thinking about and working on *Black Faces, White Spaces*.

Transforming the research into a book proved to be a challenging task that at times threatened to get the best of me, particularly while trying to learn the ropes in my new assistant professorship position at the University of California, Berkeley. So I have to thank my colleagues in the Department of Environmental Science, Policy, and Management for providing insight and the "extra" push that I sometimes needed. Specifically, I want to thank Carolyn Merchant and Nancy Peluso for taking the time to read my manuscript, offer me sound advice, and cheering me on. I am forever indebted to Denise Leto, who, as my developmental editor, was kind, sharp, and kept me laughing in the moments when I needed it. I also want to thank the graduate students who have taken my class and continue to remind me of what it means to walk my talk in my work and in my life.

One of the great joys of writing this book has been having the chance to meet so many hard-working and thoughtful people at the National Park Service. At a time of great change in the United States, these women and men are working to find ways to nurture and support healthy relationships between all peoples and the national parks. I want to give a very big "thank you" to past and current NPS directors, Robert Stanton and Jon Jarvis, respectively; park rangers Bill Gwaltney, Brenda Lanzendorf, Shelton Johnson, Betty Reid Soskin, and numerous others who made me feel welcome, shared their experiences, and revealed the magic of the parks they worked in. I continue to be humbled by your love and commitment to our national parks.

I have had the privilege of working with individuals from a variety of environmental organizations who are taking the time to envision and create new possibilities. Perhaps the organization that has had the greatest impact on me is the Center for Whole Communities in Vermont. Founders Peter Forbes and Helen Whybrow and Executive Director Ginny McGinn have created a space where people from many different walks of life come together to talk, dream, and consider new ways to be in community with each other on the land on which we live. I am so thankful for being allowed to be a part of this effort.

I continue to discover and be amazed at all the work that goes into making a book an in-your-hands reality. So I must thank everyone at UNC Press for bringing their skills and energy to this process. At the top of that list is my editor, Mark Simpson-Vos. From the moment of our first conversation, I knew I had hit the jackpot. The care, thoughtfulness, and creativity that he has brought to my first experience of writing a book has made even the most difficult moments (and yes, there were a few!) doable. While he has challenged me, he has never tried to change my writing voice. Instead, he has given me room to fly. He has, simply put, made me a better writer.

I would also like to thank all the anonymous reviewers who took the time to read my manuscript and share their insights with me. Your thoughts and ideas egged me on in necessary and often unexpected ways.

I had the good fortune to be in the same place at the same time as artist Miguel Arzabe whose artwork is on the cover of my book. Thank you for your vision and generosity and talent—I had a wish, and you made it come true.

What would my experience have been like without amazing friends and colleagues? Kaylynn TwoTrees, Julian Agyeman, Rashad Shabazz, Celine Pallud, Nina Roberts, Rue Mapp, Valerie Boyd, Matt Kolan, Noriko Ishiyama, Jun Kamata, Bev Colston, Marla Emory, Marcelo Bonta, Lauret Savoy, Marguerite Brown—at various stages in this process, you all have provided me with ideas, laughter, friendship, support, food, fun, wisdom, and love. I am forever grateful for knowing you all.

When I began this research, I needed to find a place to start. So I googled "African Americans and the environment" to see what popped up. What I got was an amazing woman who started off as my "community partner" in this work and who has become one of my best friends. Audrey Peterman epitomizes generosity, exuberance, and what it means to commit to something beyond one's self. She connected me to so many incredible people that I was able to interview, brought me food when I needed it (the best jerk chicken, *ever*), and reminded me of who I am and what I'm capable of, especially in my lowest moments.

I am forever indebted to all the people who gave me the great privilege of hearing their stories. While I cannot list everyone that I spoke to, I do want to mention four people who expanded my world and the possibilities of what could be: John Francis (planet walker), MayVynee Betsch ("I am the freest person you will ever meet"), Brenda Palms Barber (Bees in the hood), and Tyree Guyton (Detroit artist). I see in you, not just what is possible for black people, but what is possible for all people, if we only dare.

I must acknowledge those African Americans whose words, art, and lives have influenced my own: Alice Walker, Zora Neale Hurston, Bernice Johnson Reagan, Toni Morrison, Spike Lee, Malcolm X, Dr. Martin Luther King, and so many more. The world is brighter, deeper, and richer because of your presence. Thank you.

Finally, I would like to thank my parents and my brothers. We had the great privilege of caring for and living on that very special piece of land. I had—I have—the greatest privilege of being able to call you my family. My heart is full. This book is for you. I love you.

I fear that I have not remembered to mention everyone here. Please forgive me and know that if I have not mentioned your name, it is due to my shortcomings as a human being and not the value and magic of your contribution. It lives on in these pages.

Index

National Underground Railroad Network to Freedom, 101, 143 (n. 11)

Nation-building, 11, 42, 43, 130, 138; African American marginalization and exclusion from, 17–18, 39; wilderness and, 50

Native Americans, 22, 26, 41, 49–50, 58, 74–75, 81

Nature, xv, 4, 7, 8, 28, 33, 48, 56; African American relationship to, 17, 38–39, 79; history of human relationship with, 23–24, 141 (n. 4); and "Mother Nature," 144 (n. 1); and race, 38–39, 130; and society, 77. *See also* Environment

Neal, Sarah, 42

Nelson, Stanley, Sr., 51

The New Countryside?: Ethnicity, Nation and Exclusion in Contemporary Rural Britain (Neal and Agyeman), 42

New Orleans, La., 39, 67, 144 (n. 2)

Newsweek (magazine), 50

New York Post (newspaper), 32

New York Times (newspaper), 51, 60–61, 123

Northlawn Employment Network, 125–26

Obama, Barack, 32, 33, 42, 145 (n. 9)

On Land, Race, Power, and Privilege (Center for Whole Communities), 112

Outdoor recreation, African American participation in, 2, 8–9, 26–27, 29, 80, 87, 91, 131

Outka, Paul, 17, 35, 38, 39

Outside (magazine), xii, 2, 27, 78–79, 80

Overdevest, Christine, 26

Palms Barber, Brenda, 124, 125–27, 132

Parks, Rosa, 31, 46

Participant Observation, 13–14, 140 (n. 10)

Participatory Research, 13–14

Pennington, J. W. C., 62

People of Color Leadership Summit, 94

Peterman, Audrey, 67, 79, 89, 104–5, 108, 112, 147 (n. 53)

The Philadelphia Negro (Du Bois), 96

Pinchot, Gifford, 37, 39

Pinkney, Bill, 113

Pollard, Ingrid, 69–70

Post Traumatic Slave Syndrome (PTSS), 116, 118

Prejudice, 29, 31, 89, 93–94

Preservation, 4, 12, 36, 37

Preservation (magazine), 88

Primate Visions (Haraway), 32, 33

Race, xv, 20, 28–29, 96; as contested concept, 52, 95; and food, 7; massacres related to, 37; and natural environment, 2, 15, 38–39, 130

Race and Nature (Outka), 38, 39

Race Matters (West), 98

Racialization, 2, 3, 7; of environment, 4–5, 10, 35, 68, 79; national parks and, 16, 28; and representation, 10, 42–43, 67–68, 74–75, 81–82, 130

Racism, 8, 19, 93–97, 105; contrasting views on, 97–98; definition, 93; divisiveness and violence spawned by, 94, 148 (n. 2); environmental justice movement as vehicle for confronting, xiii; environmental movement and, 19–20, 92, 100–101, 113–15; and prejudice, 93–94; scientific veneer given to, 39–42

Randall, Alice, 74

Reagan, Bernice Johnson, xvii–xviii, 139 (n. 3)

Reparations movement, 24

Representation, 71–74, 131; blacks' relationship to environment affected by, 11, 86; of environment, 2, 4–5, 10, 27, 68–69; Hurricane Katrina and, 67–68, 144–45 (n. 2); and identity, 6, 69–70, 76–77, 145 (n. 3); media images and, 17, 32–33, 42, 70–71, 87, 91; and misrepresentation, 72–74; national parks and, 16, 28, 81–82, 83, 85–86; and power, 3, 7, 68; racialized, 10, 42–43, 67–68, 74–75, 81–82, 130; and stereotypes, 19, 72; of wilderness, 27, 76–77, 90–91. *See also* Stereotypes

The River (film), 77–78, 145 (n. 10)

Rock Creek Park (Washington, D.C.), 61

Wolch, Jennifer, 40
Workforce Diversity Management, 101
World's fairs, 39, 42–43
Worster, Donald, 5, 16, 56
Wright, Richard, 116, 118
Wright Museum of African American
	History, 34–35

The Year of the Gorilla (Schaller), 45
Yellowstone Park, 99
Yosemite, 28–29, 37, 82–83
Young, Andrew, 44

Zahniser, Howard, 44, 47
Zimmermann, George, 150 (n. 1)

CPSIA information can be obtained
at www.ICGtesting.com
Printed in the USA
BVHW030841121121
621447BV00028B/273